EYEWITNESS
# THE AMAZON

Yellow poison
arrow frog

Fungus
beetle

Hercules
beetle

Cinnamon
sticks

Souvenir mask
made from
natural rubber

Blue morpho
butterfly

Golden tegu

Amazon River

# EYEWITNESS
# THE
# AMAZON

Written by
## TOM JACKSON

Paradise
tanager

Macaw

Golden lion tamarin

Green-billed
toucan

**Green and black poison dart frog**

**Consultant** John Woodward

**DK D**ELHI
**Project editor** Bharti Bedi
**Editor** Priyaneet Singh
**Art editor** Pooja Pipil
**Design team** Tanvi Sahu, Nidhi Rastogi, Nishesh Batnagar
**DTP designers** Nityanand Kumar, Pawan Kumar
**Picture researcher** Aditya Katyal
**Jacket designer** Suhita Dharamjit
**Managing jackets editor** Saloni Talwar
**Pre-production manager** Balwant Singh
**Production manager** Pankaj Sharma
**Managing editor** Kingshuk Ghoshal
**Managing art editor** Govind Mittal

**DK L**ONDON
**Senior editor** Chris Hawkes
**Senior art editor** Spencer Holbrook
**US senior editor** Margaret Parrish
**Jacket editor** Claire Gell
**Jacket designer** Laura Brim
**Jacket design development manager** Sophia MTT
**Producer, pre-production** Luca Frassinetti
**Producer** Gemma Sharpe
**Managing editor** Linda Esposito
**Managing art editor** Philip Letsu
**Publisher** Andrew Macintyre
**Publishing director** Jonathan Metcalf
**Associate publishing director** Liz Wheeler
**Design director** Stuart Jackman

First American Edition, 2015

Published in the United States by DK Publishing
345 Hudson Street, New York, New York 10014

A Penguin Random House Company

15 16 17 18 19 10 9 8 7 6 5 4 3 2 1
001—280097—June/15

Published in Great Britain by Dorling Kindersley Limited.

A catalog record for this book is available from the
Library of Congress.

ISBN 978-1-4654-3566-8 (Paperback)
ISBN 978-1-4654-3567-5 (ALB)

DK books are available at special discounts when
purchased in bulk for sales promotions, premiums,
fund-raising, or educational use. For details, contact:
DK Publishing Special Markets, 345 Hudson Street,
New York, New York 10014 or SpecialSales@dk.com.

Printed by South China Printing Co. Ltd., China

A WORLD OF IDEAS:
**SEE ALL THERE IS TO KNOW**

**www.dk.com**

Pineapple

Passion
fruit

Ocelot

Vine snake

Palm oil
and fruits

Amazonian
children on
a traditional
canoe

# Contents

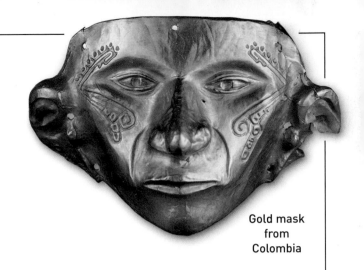

Gold mask from Colombia

# The Amazon

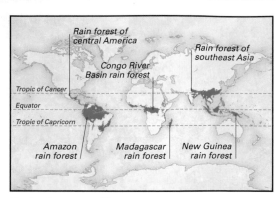

The Amazon is the site of the world's largest rain forest and its biggest river system. The Amazon rain forest contains some large cities, and ancient settlements also exist deeper in the jungle. The amazing wildlife and geography and a wealth of culture—ancient and modern—make the region one of Earth's greatest treasures.

## Rain forest climate

The Amazon, like all rain forests around the world, is in a region called the tropics—the land that lies between the Tropics of Cancer and Capricorn. In the tropics, it is hot all year round, and it rains a lot. Parts of the Amazon rain forest get just over 8 ft (2.5 m) of rain every year. All this heat and water make it possible for dense jungles to grow.

## A sight to see

Tourists visit the Amazon rain forest to see its wildlife and amazing scenery. Tourism is one of the most important industries in this rain forest. It is a good way for the local people to make money without having to clear the forest to make way for farms and factories.

Toco toucan

Black caiman

Blue morpho butterfly

Agouti

## Modern cities

The Amazon rain forest contains several big cities. Iquitos, in Peru, is one of the largest. It is home to 420,000 people, and it is just like any modern city—with parks, movie theaters, and a sports stadium. The main difference is that the city is surrounded by the rain forest and there are no highways linking it to the next town. The things people need to live arrive in ships sailing up the Amazon River.

Scarlet macaw

Tree crown

Blue and yellow macaw

**It's a jungle out there**
The Amazon rain forest is one of the most diverse habitats on Earth. One in 10 of the world's animal and plant species lives in its forests and rivers. Some animals, such as monkeys, seldom leave the tangle of branches, while plenty more live beside the shallow rivers. Others spend their entire lives on the forest floor.

Howler monkey

Three-toed sloth

Emerald tree boa

Giant otter

Capybara

Giant lily pad

Green iguana

Jaguar

# The Amazon Basin

The Amazon rain forest exists because of South America's unique climate and geography. Storms from the Atlantic Ocean travel inland to produce rain on a vast, bowl-shaped area known as the Amazon Basin. Like a sink, or basin, in a bathroom, it collects the rain that falls into it. Some of that water feeds the rain forest; the rest gushes into rivers that join to form the Amazon River.

*Ridge of mountain peaks surrounds the Amazon Basin*

## Expansive region

The Amazon Basin covers 40 percent of South America. The basin is surrounded by a wall of hills and mountains. Every drop of rain that falls inside this wall enters the Amazon River system.

*ATLANTIC OCEAN*

Kaieteur Falls= ▲ Mount Roraima
Angel Falls= ▲ Auyen Tepui

Llanos

Rio Negro

Rio Japura

Amazon

Rio Putumayo

Rio Purus

2

6

Manaus

5

Amazon

• Iquitos

Rio Jurua

Rio Ucayali

8

Volcan Sangay ▲ ▲
Volcan Cotopaxi

Yerupaja ▲

**A N D E S**

*PACIFIC OCEAN*

## At the mouth

The Amazon has the largest mouth of any river—about a fifth of all the river water in the world enters the Atlantic Ocean through it. This water carries immense amounts of sediment, which eventually settles at the bottom of the ocean. That forms an area of seabed called the Amazon Cone, which reaches about 435 miles (700 km) from the coast.

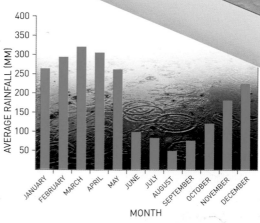

400
350
300
250
200
150
100
50

AVERAGE RAINFALL (MM)

JANUARY FEBRUARY MARCH APRIL MAY JUNE JULY AUGUST SEPTEMBER OCTOBER NOVEMBER DECEMBER

MONTH

## Rainfall

The Amazon Basin receives an average of 7½ ft (2.3 m) of rainfall every year. However, this rain is not spread evenly. Most of it falls between November and May.

## Kaieteur Falls

Most of the Amazon Basin is very flat, so waterfalls and rapids are rare. The biggest waterfall inside the Basin is the Kaieteur Falls in the Guiana Highlands. Here, the water drops from a height of 741 ft (226 m), more than four times the height of the Niagara Falls. This waterfall carries a massive 23,400 cu ft per second (663 cu meters per second) of water.

### KEY

— BASIN BOUNDARY
● CITY
═ WATERFALL
▲ MOUNTAIN

lém
**10**
**7**
Rio Tocantins
Rio Araguaia
Rio Xingu
● Brasília
**Mato Grosso**
*Atlantic Forest*
● Rio de Janeiro
● Sao Paulo
Pantanal
to Velho
*Iguazu Falls*═
Rio Mamore
● LA PAZ
**3**
Lake Titicaca
▲ Volcan Tutupaca
Salar de Uyuni
● Machu Picchu
**A N D E S**
Atacama Desert

*Soil has a reddish tinge because of its iron content*

## Basin soil

Even though the world's largest rain forest grows out of it, the soil in the Amazon Basin is surprisingly thin and does not contain many nutrients. Most fertile soils are filled with organic material that forms from the remains of dead plants and animals. This is not the case in the Amazon region. Here, fungi and bacteria recycle these substances so quickly that they are absorbed immediately by the roots of living plants.

## POINTS OF INTEREST

**1** TIDAL BORE
A wave up to 13 ft (4 m) high that rushes upriver at high tide.

**2** MEETING OF THE WATERS
The Rio Negro's dark waters meet the muddy Amazon River here.

**3** NEVADO MISMI
The source of the Amazon River in the Peruvian Andes.

**4** NAZCA LINES
Ancient patterns cut into the desert by the Nazca people.

**5** LÁBREA
One end of the Trans-Amazonian Highway (runs through the forest).

**6** RIO NEGRO BRIDGE
The first major road bridge to cross a river in the region.

**7** CARAJÁS MINE
The largest iron ore mine in the world.

**8** KUELAP
An ancient fortress built by the Chachapoya people.

**9** MARAJÓ ISLAND
The largest river island in the world.

**10** TUCURUÍ DAM
A huge power plant built across the Rio Tocantins.

## Drought in the basin

These fishermen from Marajó Island, on the Amazon River, have nowhere to paddle their boat. In July and August, the water level around the Amazon River's mouth drops because of less rain farther upstream.

# The Amazon River

The Amazon River is the largest river in the world—it is twice as large as its nearest rival, the Congo in Central Africa. The water flows from west to east and eventually divides to form a huge 202-mile- (325-km-) wide estuary near Macapá, Brazil. Here, the river empties enough water into the Atlantic Ocean to fill 5,000 Olympic swimming pools every minute.

*A wooden cross marks the Amazon River's source*

### The source

The Amazon River's source is Nevado Mismi in the mountains of Peru. From here, meltwater flows through the mountains into the Amazon and on to the Atlantic. The Amazon is commonly thought to be 4,049 miles (6,516 km) long, second in length only to the Nile in Africa, although some scientists believe it could be longer.

### Meeting of the waters

The Amazon River's largest tributary is the Rio Negro, or black river. Its water is filled with chemicals washed out of soil and plants, which make it very dark. It joins the Amazon near the Brazilian city of Manaus, but the waters of the two rivers do not mix for a few miles, creating a two-tone river.

### The river sea

The Amazon contains so much water that it is more like a sea than a river. The main channel is about 165 ft (50 m) deep and can be more than 6 miles (10 km) wide when flooded by heavy rains.

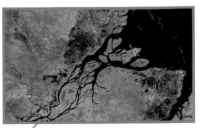

A satellite image of the
mouth of the Amazon River

## Great roar

Top surfers come to ride the Amazon River's
tidal bore—a wave created in the river's wide
mouth by the ocean tides. Twice a day, water
from the Atlantic surges up the river, reversing
its flow. When the tide is high and the river
level is low, a 13-ft- (4-m-) high wave rushes
up the river, traveling up to 500 miles (800 km)
upstream. The Brazilian name for the wave
is the *pororoca*, or "great roar."

Rio Negro

*Amazon*

Amazon River

*Basin*

Rio Madeira

Rio Tapajós

Rio Xingu

Rio Tocantins

Rio Ucayali

## Many branches

The Amazon River
flows from Peru to the
Atlantic coast of Brazil.
Along the way, it is joined
by about 1,100 tributaries,
many of which are huge rivers.
The Madeira, Negro, and Paraná
Rivers, for example, each carry more
water than any river in Europe or North
America. At its mouth, the Amazon again
splits into several channels, creating the
world's largest river islands; the biggest,
Marajó, is roughly the size of Switzerland.

## Mixing with the ocean

When it reaches the sea, the Amazon River's muddy
freshwater flows 250 miles (400 km) out into the
Atlantic. The tucuxi, an Amazon River dolphin, also
follows the river out to sea. Some groups of tucuxi
have even been found living near Rio de Janeiro,
more than 1,500 miles (2,500 km) to the south.

# Land of forests

The Amazon Basin contains the world's largest tropical forest—10 times the size of Spain. Most of the basin is covered in lowland rain forest, which gets plenty of rain, so the trees here grow faster and taller than anywhere else in the Amazon rain forest. This region is also home to other types of forest, depending on climate and geography.

**Palm**
Along the southern edge of the Amazon rain forest, where it is a little drier, the forest is dominated by palm trees. The most common type of palm is the babassu, which local people use both as a building material and as a source of food.

**Woody vines**
Lianas are thick, woody vines that grow up from the ground using the branches of trees to support them. Once it reaches sunlight, a liana spreads out, running from tree to tree, sprouting leafy branches. A liana forest grows in places in which trees are widely spaced, and the vines can fill the gaps between them. It is most common in the hills to the south of the Amazon River's mouth.

**Dry forests**
The arid highland areas around the edge of the Amazon rain forest are covered in caatinga, meaning "white forest" in the local language—a reference to the area's dry, sandy soil. Only small trees and thorny shrubs can grow here. Other areas that are too dry for full forests are covered in cerrado, the Brazilian word for savanna.

**Underwater roots**
After heavy rains, river levels in the Amazon can rise by several yards, leading to flooding in large parts of the rain forest. Roots need air to function well, so trees in a flooded forest do not grow as tall as in other areas, since their roots are submerged.

### Seeds in water

The rubber plant times the release of its seeds—which float—for when the water is at its highest. The seeds are a source of food for many fish, but those that are not eaten are washed far and wide and grow into new trees when the water goes down.

### Cloud forest

Mountain forests are known as "cloud forests," as they are often shrouded in thick fog. The weather on mountain slopes is different from that in the lowlands: it rains less, and the temperature is lower. The trees there do not grow tall and are often covered in mosses and creepers.

### Near the Atlantic

A woolly spider monkey can be seen climbing a vine in the Atlantic Forest on the Brazilian Highlands, near the Atlantic Ocean. A band of hills cuts off this area from the main Amazon Basin. Much of the wildlife found here is unique to this region. The area is also one of the most deforested zones in South America, and many of its animals are endangered.

# Around the rain forest

The Amazon Basin is surrounded on three sides by mountains. The Guiana Highlands in the north feature incredible waterfalls. To the south are the Brazilian Highlands, a huge mass of rolling hills. To the west lie the Andes—the world's longest mountain range, dotted with volcanoes.

## Wall of mountains

The Andes are about 4,350 miles (7,000 km) long and run from Venezuela in the north to the southern tip of South America. The Central Andes, which run through Ecuador, Peru, and Bolivia, are closest to the Amazon Basin. They contain several high, flat areas on which ancient civilizations, such as the Incas, once thrived.

## Floating village

The body of water shown here is Lake Titicaca, South America's largest freshwater lake. Nestled nearly 2.5 miles (4 km) above sea level in the Andes, it is inhabited by the Uru people, who live in floating houses.

## Salt flat

Ten cities the size of Paris could fit inside the Salar de Uyuni—the world's largest salt flat. Located in the Bolivian Andes, it was formed when a prehistoric lake dried out, leaving behind a layer of salt. It is also the flattest place on Earth.

*Flat summit is covered in rocks and pools of rainwater*

Cracked crust covers lower layers of salty slush

## Table mountain

At a height of 9,219 ft (2,810 m), Mount Roraima is one of the highest points in the Guiana Highlands. Two billion years old, it is made of a block of sandstone that was left behind after the softer rocks around it were washed away.

## Mountain animals

The high slopes of the Andes Mountains can be very cold and dry. Llamas survive there because they have thick wool. Like their relative the camel, they can also survive for long periods without water.

*125-ft- (38-m-) tall concrete statue*

## Crowded coast

Seen here is the statue of Christ the Redeemer looking down on Rio de Janeiro from a forested peak. This city, which is home to about 12 million people, is one of the largest cities in the Brazilian Highlands and is located where the hills meet the Atlantic Ocean.

# Wetlands

In addition to the Amazon River, there are also vast wetlands that collect water in the Amazon Basin. To the south is the Pantanal, the planet's biggest swamp; to the north is Los Llanos, a grassland that turns into a huge temporary marshland once a year. These wetlands are fertile and have been important farming regions for centuries. They also contain unique animals, such as the saberfin killifish and the Orinoco crocodile.

Long, flexible neck

Anhinga

### Waterways
Water flowing from the hills around the Pantanal collects in a wetland, where it becomes trapped in the basin and drains away through the Paraguay River. Los Llanos is fed by the yearly flooding of the Orinoco River that covers the low areas of Venezuela and Colombia for months on end.

### Spear fishing
The anhinga is a fish-hunting water bird that lives in the Pantanal. It spears its prey with its long beak and then swallows the prey whole. Its name means "snakebird" in the local language. When it is in the water, only its long neck and head are visible, making it look like a snake rising out of the water.

Thick tail

Golden tegu

Powerful jaw muscles

### Golden lizard
The golden tegu is one of the largest lizards in South America, growing to a length of 3¼ ft (1 m). It hunts for food on land and in water, and can stay underwater for around 20 minutes at a time. This reptile eats all kinds of food, from fruits to dead animals.

Llanos

Pantanal

## Pink tree

Unlike most forest trees, which are evergreens, the pink lapacho tree is deciduous—it loses its leaves seasonally. It sheds its leaves in the dry, winter months, and grows its flowers before the leaves return in spring. This makes it look pink and attracts pollinators such as hummingbirds.

## Terena

Seen here is an archer at Brazil's Indigenous Games in 2013. He is representing the Terena tribe, who have lived around the Pantanal wetland for thousands of years. Terena warriors used their weapons for real recently, as they took back their traditional lands from farmers who were using it illegally. Despite their ancient customs, they organized the campaign using Facebook.

## Cattle country

Huge herds of cattle are raised on the Pantanal and Los Llanos. Most of the wetland areas are flooded for only part of the year, so when the water recedes, lush pastures grow on the fertile soil. Cowboys—known as *Pantaneiros* in the Pantanal and *Llaneros* in Los Llanos—look after the cattle herds in these pastures.

*Pantaneiros*

## Giant lily pads

The Victoria lilies of the Pantanal have pads about 8¼ ft (2.5 m) wide, which makes them the largest leaves in the world. Although they are fragile, the pads can support the weight of small animals, such as frogs and birds, if their weight is spread evenly. The lily's large flowers also float on the surface. They are pollinated by beetles that fly from one bloom to the other.

# Plants and fungi

Of the 40,000 species of plant in the Amazon rain forest, only about a third are trees. The rest include plants without roots that collect water from the air, long creepers, and even species that catch insects. This region also teems with fungi, many of which grow in the soil and turn dead leaves into vital nutrients for plants.

**Kapok**
Growing to roughly 230 ft (70 m) tall and about 10 ft (3 m) around the base, the kapok is one of the largest trees in the rain forest. Its trunk grows large buttress roots, which help support the tree.

**Plant ponds**
This poison dart frog raises its tadpole in a small pond that has formed in the base of a bromeliad plant. Bromeliads have fleshy leaves that fan out in circles, creating bowl shapes.

*Sticky liquid on soft tentacle*

*Moth stuck to leaf*

**Eating bugs**
Sundews live in swampy regions of the rain forest. Their leaves are covered in soft tentacles that are coated in sticky liquid. When an insect lands on a leaf, it becomes stuck. The leaf then curls around the insect and digests it, extracting useful nutrients.

## Symbiosis

Cecropia trees recruit an army of ants to defend them against attack. The small trees have hollow areas in their stems and branches in which the ants make their home. In return, the ants clean fungus off the leaves and attack other insects that venture on to the plant, including those that come to feed on the leaves. As a reward, the plant produces oily nodules, which the ants cut off and eat. The way in which both plant and animal benefit from one another is called symbiosis.

*Cecropia ant carrying oily nodule produced by plant*

## Up in the air

About a quarter of rain forest plants do not grow a long stem or trunk to reach sunlight. Instead, they grow on bigger plants above the ground. These plants—called epiphytes—have leaves, flowers, and fruits, but no true roots. They get the water they need from the moisture in the air.

*Spores fall out of cap as tiny, cup-shaped mushroom dries out*

## Strangler fig

This network of stems (above) once contained a tree trunk. The stems belong to a strangler fig, a plant that grows from a seed at the top of a tall tree. The roots grow down to the ground to get water and nutrients and end up encircling the tree trunk. Eventually, the tree inside dies under the weight of the fig and rots away.

## Forest mushrooms

Fungi are key waste recyclers in the forest. These mushrooms (right) are growing on and inside the dead wood, helping it to rot away and release nutrients into the soil.

# Birds of the Amazon

Around 1,500 bird species live in the Amazon rain forest. They range from macaws—the world's biggest parrots—to tiny hummingbirds. Many water birds also live in the region's vast wetlands and along its riverbanks. Forest birds have plenty of places to hide, but the males can use their bright plumage when they want to be seen, especially when they want to attract mates.

Green-billed toucan

## Long bill
The toucan's long, chunky bill makes up about a quarter of its body length. However, the bill is light   and is made of a spongy bone covered in a coat of keratin, the material found in a human's fingernails. The bill has rough edges that are useful for cracking nuts and peeling fruits. Toucans rarely fly far, preferring to hop from branch to branch.

## Hovering to feed
Although it weighs only 0.03 oz (9 g) and is just 6 in (15 cm) long, the swallowtail hummingbird is the largest hummingbird in the Amazon. Living at the mid-level of the rain forest, its wings beat at a rate of 50 times a second, allowing it to hover in front of a flower while sipping the nectar with its long tongue.

## High fliers
Brightly colored macaws flying high above the trees are easy to notice. These large birds eat unripe fruits that most forest animals ignore, as the macaw's hooked beak can rip away the tough outer layers of the fruits. They also often gather in large flocks on muddy riverbanks, where they lick the soil to get the salts and nutrients missing in their food.

## Laughing falcon

This bird of prey with a high-pitched cackle perches above a clearing and looks for prey on the ground. When it spots a victim, such as a snake, it swoops down and lands on top of it. It kills its victims with a quick bite to the back of the head.

*Coral snake*

*Tail makes up more than half the bird's length*

*Bright plumage*

## Hanging nests

These bags of woven grasses and twigs are the nests of oropendolas—songbirds that eat insects and fruits. Each nest cluster is a breeding colony ruled by a single male, who mates with most of the females there. The female lays two eggs at the bottom of the nest, and her chicks learn to fly about a month after hatching.

*Adults have a crest of spiked feathers*

## Stinkbird

The strange hoatzin ferments meals of fruits and leaves in a bloated stomach filled with bacteria. Local people call it the stinkbird, because its digestion produces bad odors. Hoatzin chicks are born with claws on their wings, which they use to climb through branches before learning to fly.

## Fishing for food

The boat-billed heron is one of the many water birds that live in the Amazon rain forest. It uses its long legs to wade through shallow water when looking for food. It scoops up food using its wide, shovel-shaped bill, which helps it to feel for prey in the mud and among the weeds. The heron shown here is about to feast on a fish, but this species also eats shellfish, water voles, and birds' eggs.

## Colorful songbird

Feeding on insects, paradise tanagers are little songbirds that live in the forest canopy, far above the ground. Although tanagers can be difficult to spot, the males are brightly colored so that they can get noticed by mates. They show off their plumes by performing a bowing dance on a perch. By contrast, the females tend to stay out of sight, building small, cup-shaped nests hidden among the leaves.

# Amazon monkeys

Some 130 species of monkey live in the Amazon rain forest, eating leaves, fruits, and insects. The monkeys of the Amazon belong to a group called New World monkeys that descended from African monkeys. Unlike their Old World relatives, Amazon monkeys have flat noses with nostrils that point sideways. Many species also have a flexible tail that can work as a hand or foot to wrap around branches and grip objects.

*Adult marmosets are only 5 in (12 cm) long*

### Agile climber

Named after the way it looks when it hangs from its strong tail, the spider monkey lives at the top of tall trees and almost never comes to the ground. They gather in troops of about 30, and work together to protect a feeding territory, seeking out food such as fruits, leaves, and even birds' eggs.

### Mini monkey

The pygmy marmoset is the tiniest monkey in the world. It lives in small bushes that grow along riverbanks and the edge of the forest. Its main food is sap—a sweet, sticky liquid made by plants.

*Hair on forehead can be raised*

Brown capuchin monkey

*Hard nut cracked open with stone*

### Clever capuchins

There are nine species of capuchin monkey in the Amazon rain forest. They are highly intelligent and are known to use simple tools, such as stones, to crack open nuts and a sponge of mashed-up leaves to soak up fruit juices. The capuchin monkeys were given their name because their brown fur and the dark "cap" on their head reminded early European explorers of Capuchin monks.

Capuchin monk

## Loud howler

Howler monkeys are not only the largest and noisiest monkeys in the Amazon rain forest, but also the loudest land animals. Their calls can travel up to 2.5 miles (4 km) through the forest. They use their large, flexible throats to boost their volume when calling from the treetops. Males do most of the calling, to attract females or to warn other males to stay away.

*Howler monkeys can grow up to 35 in (90 cm) tall*

*Dark and hairless face*

## Nocturnal monkey

The douroucoulis, or owl monkeys, are the only monkey species in the world that is nocturnal, or active at night. Their huge eyes allow them to see well enough in the dark to run and jump through the branches. They move around in small family groups, and if one monkey sees a predator, such as a snake, it will give out a long "wook" call to warn the others.

*Large eyes only see in black-and-white*

## Lion's mane

The flowing mane of a golden lion tamarin resembles the mane of a lion. These brightly colored monkeys live in the dense, hot, and humid jungles of the Atlantic Forest. They are most active in the cool mornings and evenings and take naps during the middle of the day. These tamarins live in groups of about eight. Only the chief male and female breed, while the other group members help them raise their young.

23

# On the forest floor

Not all animals in the Amazon rain forest live in trees—many species, including the giant armadillo and the peccary, also live on the forest floor. The thick covering of trees means very little sunlight reaches the ground. There is not much wind down there either, and the moisture in the air makes it very humid.

## Flatworm

Most of the world's flatworms live in water, but it is so humid in the Amazon rain forest that some, such as the Amazonian land planarian (above), slither around on the ground. If it is bitten in half by a predator, a new worm will grow back from each half.

*Circles of pale fur around eyes look like eyeglasses*

## Giant armadillo

The Amazon's giant armadillo—the world's largest species of armadillo—can grow up to 5 ft (1.5 m) long. This forest giant forages at night and digs its way into termite mounds and ant nests using long claws on its forelegs. It licks up the insects inside using a long, sticky tongue.

*Tough, dark brown shell composed of bony plates*

## Spectacled bear

The spectacled bear is the only bear species in the Amazon rain forest. It is not a fierce hunter. During the day, it prefers to sleep in a cave or hollow tree. At night, it climbs through low branches, feeding on fruits, lush leaves, and any insects and rodents it can catch.

*Long claws help to grip while climbing*

## Pack hunters

Bush dogs are related to wolves. They work in packs of around 12 to chase rodents and ground birds through the forest. They make squeaking calls to keep track of each other among the thick undergrowth.

## Peccaries

Even though it resembles a wild boar, the white-lipped peccary is only distantly related to pigs. Moving through the forest in herds of more than 100, it uses its flexible snout to find roots, mushrooms, and rotting fruits to eat.

## Deadly viper

The lancehead is a venomous viper that lies hidden among fallen leaves and strikes quickly when prey, such as a rodent, walks past. Its venom does not kill straight away. If its prey runs away, the snake tracks its victim using heat-sensitive pits on its snout.

*Arrow-shaped head gives the snake its name*

*Exposed tip of the tail may help lure prey when the viper is hidden on the forest floor*

## Jungle cat

The ocelot may look like a leopard, but it is not much bigger than a domestic cat. During the day it sleeps on a shady branch, but at night it hunts, mostly on the ground, tracking small prey, such as opossums, mice, and frogs, by their smell. It has excellent night vision.

*Long whiskers help the ocelot to feel its way around*

# Creepy-crawlies

Insects, spiders, worms, and other invertebrates make up almost 95 percent of all animal species in the Amazon rain forest. One survey confirmed that about 50,000 insect species live in every 1 sq mile (2.59 sq km) of the rain forest. Scientists have also calculated that ants, wasps, and termites equal more than half of the total weight of animals in the Amazon. So, put together, they far outweigh all the big vertebrates, such as mammals, birds, and reptiles.

## Hard-working ants

Eating around half a million insects a day, an army ant colony of more than a million ants spreads out in a column 330 ft (100 m) long. The worker ants use their bodies to build shelters or to make a bridge over an obstacle, as seen here.

## Startling cricket

A katydid is a type of cricket: this one (right) is known as a peacock katydid. It has a green body, and its wings look like a drying leaf. If a predator were to spot it, this insect might open its wings wide like a peacock to reveal bright "eyespots" to startle the attacker.

*Eyespot on wing*

Titan beetle

Metallic wood boring beetle

Fungus beetle

Hercules beetle

## Beetle mania

Beetles are the most common type of insect, and the Amazon rain forest has more than its fair share of them. It is home to the titan beetle, which is 6¼ in (16 cm) long and has mouthparts strong enough to cut through a pencil. At up to 6¾ in (17 cm), the Hercules beetle is even longer.

### Winged beauty

The Amazon rain forest has at least 3,000 butterfly species, the most vibrant of which are the shimmering morphos. An owl butterfly tries to stay hidden, but if a predator closes in, the big butterfly opens its wings to show two large eyespots that make it look like the face of a scary owl.

Owl butterfly

Blue morpho butterfly

### Mimic

The thorax (mid-body) of the praying mantis looks more like a plant than an insect. This helps the mantis stay hidden from predators, such as frogs and birds, and also makes the insect invisible to its prey.

*Hind wings resemble folded leaves*

### Monster centipede

The Amazon giant centipede is one of the largest centipedes in the world. At about 10 in (25 cm) long, it hunts all over the rain forest, using its 36 or more clawed feet to climb in the trees. With its powerful venom, it preys on many animals, including snakes and birds. It even crawls into caves to kill bats as they sleep hanging from the roof.

Jumping spider

*Vein pattern similar to that of a leaf*

Goliath bird-eating spider

### Eight-legged giant

The Amazon's Goliath bird-eating spider is as large as a dinner plate, but it mainly eats earthworms. The region is also home to the tiny jumping spider which, amazingly, can jump 30 times its own body length.

# In and around the river

Several animals that are more common in the ocean have made their homes in the rivers of the Amazon Basin. For example, there are dolphins living in the flooded forests of Peru and Ecuador, 1,865 miles (3,000 km) from the ocean. Some unusual animals also live on the riverbanks, including tapirs, which are South America's closest relatives to the horse.

**River mermaid**

The Amazonian manatee looks like a seal, but it is an aquatic relative of the elephant. Some manatees—although not this species—live in the ocean, and legend has it that lonely sailors mistook them for mermaids.

*Flippers help the Amazonian manatee to steer in the water*

## Giant rodent

The order of animals known as rodents includes small animals such as mice and squirrels. At 4¼ ft (1.3 m) long and weighing as much as an adult human, the capybara is the world's largest rodent. Its sharp front teeth can slice through plant stems. Capybaras live in herds that graze together on lush riverbanks.

Thick fur keeps out water

Eyes on top of the head help the capybara to stay alert even when it is almost completely submerged in water

Barrel-shaped body contains a large gut that is ideal for digesting plants

Feet are partially webbed, which helps when swimming

Flexible snout helps to sniff out food, water, and mates

Rump

## Brazilian tapir

At 6½ ft (2 m) long, the tapir (left) is the largest land animal in the Amazon rain forest. During the day, it stays hidden in dense bushes. At night, it comes out to graze on the riverbank and take a swim, wallowing in the shallow water.

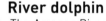

## River dolphin

The Amazon River dolphin, or boto, spends most of the year in the wide, deep rivers. In the rainy season, the rivers flood parts of the forest, and the dolphins follow the water to feed among the tree trunks.

Wide hooves make it easier to walk on soft mud

## Giant otter

Measuring up to 4½ ft (1.4 m) long, the Amazonian giant otter is the largest otter in the world. Large webbed feet and a long flattened tail make it a very powerful swimmer. Because it is not very agile on land, this species seldom ventures far from the riverbank.

## Yapok

A relative of Australia's kangaroos and koalas, the yapok is an aquatic marsupial—a mammal that carries its babies in a pouch and that spends much of its time in the water. The yapok's pouch is watertight, so the young do not drown.

# Hunting for food

The Amazon rain forest teems with deadly hunters—on the ground, in the water, and in the treetops. They include not only big cats, massive alligators, and giant snakes, but also the world's deadliest spiders, birds big enough to kill monkeys, and a bat that can suck your blood as you sleep.

*Front legs raised during attack*

### Deadly hunter
Although most spiders are harmless to humans, the Brazilian wandering spider is the most dangerous spider on Earth. In the absence of treatment, its venom could kill a person in 30 minutes. This deadly spider chases mice on the forest floor or frogs among the leaves, killing them in seconds with a single bite.

*Flat snout used to feel for warm skin*

### Bloodsucker
Named after Count Dracula, the vampire bat comes out to feed on dark, moonless nights. It lands near sleeping mammals, including humans, and crawls over their bodies searching for a warm patch of skin. It then makes a tiny cut with its pointed fangs and drinks the blood that flows out.

### Giant snake
At up to 16½ ft (5 m) long, the green anaconda—the world's largest snake—spends most of its time in shallow water, ready to ambush prey that wanders too close to the water's edge. The anaconda shown here has captured a caiman—another fearsome predator. The snake kills its victim by squeezing it so tightly that it stops breathing. And like all snakes, it swallows its prey headfirst and whole.

### Night stalker

The jaguar is the Amazon rain forest's largest predator, and is usually a lone, nocturnal hunter. It leaps on its prey, such as tapirs and caimans, from above, killing them with a skull-crushing bite. By day, the jaguar snoozes on a shaded branch. The fur's pattern helps the jaguar blend in to its environment.

*6½-ft- (2-m-) wide wingspan*

### On the wing

The harpy eagle is the largest bird of prey in the Amazon rain forest. It perches high up in the forest, and when it spots its prey, it swoops down and grabs its victim with its huge talons. This eagle often captures monkeys, killing them with a bite from its hooked beak, and carries them back to its perch. It also dives to the forest floor to grab ground mammals, and chases smaller birds through the trees, plucking them out of the air.

*Talons are the longest among all eagles*

*Head thrown back to swallow small prey whole*

### Killer caiman

The Amazon rain forest's caiman (a type of alligator) can grow up to 20 ft (6 m) long. They lie in shallow water and when land animals, such as peccaries, come too close, they pull them under the water and drown them. They will also attack fish and birds on the water's surface.

*Short, stocky legs are good for swimming and climbing*

# Of both worlds

Frogs, toads, and salamanders are amphibians—animals that live in water and on land. Yet, most amphibians cannot survive for long without water, which is abundant in the Amazon rain forest. A huge range of amphibians thrive there—from wormlike creatures that burrow through damp soil, to frogs that are poisonous to touch.

*Large eyes help to see at night*

## Salamander

As expert climbers, the Amazon rain forest's salamanders have webbed feet to grip leaves and branches. Most active at night, they catch insects with their long, sticky tongues. They lack lungs and do not breathe air; instead they absorb all the oxygen they need through their moist skin.

*Hornlike projections above the eyes*

*Pointed snout pushes through soil*

## Limbless

Although it resembles a worm or snake, this creature is a type of caecilian—a limbless amphibian that burrows through soil and eats underground insects. Strangely enough, caecilian babies feed on their mother's skin, pausing occasionally to let it grow back.

## Big mouth

One of the Amazon rain forest's largest amphibians, the horned frog can grow up to 8 in (20 cm) long. This frog hides itself in leaves, then uses its huge mouth, measuring half the size of its body, to gulp down mice, lizards, and other frogs.

## See-through

The glass frog's upper body looks green, but its belly skin has no color, making its heart, stomach, and bones clearly visible. It sleeps on large leaves, and the transparent skin lets the leaf color show through from underneath, making it hard to spot.

## Paradoxical frog

A paradox is something that seems impossible but is true. This Amazonian frog is a paradox because its tadpole, which grows up to 9 in (22 cm) long, gets smaller as it gets older. When it is an adult frog, it is a third of that size.

**Yellow poison arrow frog**

**Red poison dart frog**

**Green and black poison dart frog**

## Tree-dweller

The red-eyed tree frog (right) has long, slender legs for climbing and jumping, and its fingers and toes have round suction cups for gripping branches. Like other tree frogs, it lays its eggs on leaves overhanging a pool. When the tadpoles hatch, they fall into the water beneath.

*Bright coloration startles predators*

*Suction pads on fingers help frog to climb*

## Pretty poisonous

Poison dart frogs are named after the Amazonian hunters who use the powerful toxins in the skin of the species to make poisoned darts for killing monkeys. These toxins come from the chemicals in ants and other insects that these frogs eat. The toxic skin is brightly colored, which serves as a warning to predators to stay away.

## Unusual toad

The Suriname toad (above) spends its whole life in water. It uses its long, sensitive fingers to find small fish and other prey in the riverbed. During mating, the male loads fertilized eggs onto the female's back, where they are absorbed into the skin. Instead of tadpoles, tiny toadlets hatch from the eggs and burst out of the mother's back.

Blue poison dart frog

Amazon dart frog

Pasco poison dart frog

Imitating poison frog

# Forest reptiles

Reptiles have scaly skin and live in the warmer parts of the world. From killer crocodiles to venomous snakes, around 500 reptile species live in the tree tops and on the river beds of the Amazon rain forest. However, there are probably many more that scientists are yet to discover.

**Warning flap**

This tree-climbing anole lizard has a skin flap on its neck called a dewlap. When a predator comes too close, the lizard unfurls the flap, scaring off the predator. Males have brighter dewlaps than females, and they often flash them in and out to attract mates.

**Snorkeling turtle**

Like all reptiles, the mata mata turtle (left) breathes air. But instead of coming to the surface to breathe, this little river turtle has a flexible snout with long nostrils, which it uses like a snorkel. To eat, it waits among river plants, then opens its mouth very wide to suck in its prey, such as small fish.

**Tiny alligator**

Seen here is a baby dwarf caiman (a type of alligator). Among all crocodiles and alligators, dwarf caimans are the world's smallest, growing to little more than 4 ft (1.2 m) in length. They live in small streams and hunt for water snails, crabs, and frogs.

*Males have longer spikes than females*

**Jungle dragon**

Also known as a wood lizard, the forest dragon has a ridge of armored spikes along its back and tail. If threatened, it opens its mouth in a wide gape, revealing bright pink gums. The sudden flash of color often startles any attacker and helps the lizard to escape.

**Sensing heat**

The bright green body of the emerald tree boa helps it to blend in with the leaves. At night it hunts for mice, using heat-sensitive pits on its snout to track prey in the dark. These pits sense body heat given off by other animals.

*Heat sensitive pits are located along upper and lower lips*

## Targeting prey

The long and slender vine snake slithers through branches to reach out and grab lizards, chicks, and other prey. Unlike most other snakes, this venomous species is able to swivel its eyeballs, which helps it to spot and target its prey precisely before launching a speedy strike.

## Giant turtle

The male Arrau turtle is the Amazon rain forest's largest turtle, growing to 3 ft (1 m) long. Females bury their eggs on sandbars that are exposed in the dry season, when the water level drops. The baby turtles hatch at the start of the rainy season.

*Bulge on head contains venom glands*

*Triangular head shape*

## Ambush hunter

The eyelash viper's scales break up the shape of the snake's face, so it can hide from its prey among the leaves. The 24-in- (60-cm-) long viper wiggles the point of its tail to attract curious birds and lizards. It then ambushes them, delivering a venomous bite at lightning speed.

# Amazon fish

The many rivers found in the Amazon Basin are home to nearly 5,600 species of fish—15 percent of all the world's fish species. The water in some places does not contain much oxygen, especially when the river levels are low. As a result, even though they all have gills, some Amazon fish are able to breathe air as well.

## Feeding frenzy

A piranha only grows to about 8 in (20 cm) long, yet, despite its size, this sharp-toothed, meat-eating fish has a fearsome reputation. It is said that these fish can devour large animals, including cattle and humans, within minutes. However, these attacks are rare, and they only occur when the river level is low and the piranhas are bunched together looking for food.

## Venomous sting

Rays, like this stingray, are related to sharks, and the Amazon River is home to more than 20 species of them. Known as the ocellate river stingray, this fish defends itself with a venomous spike in its tail. However, it does not use its tail to catch prey, which includes crustaceans and snails.

## Giant fish

The arapaima is the largest freshwater fish in the world, weighing up to 450 lb (200 kg). The longest specimen ever caught was 15 ft (4.25 m) long, but most are about half that length. This giant fish has gills, but it also breathes air using a lunglike organ, taking a gulp of air every 10 minutes or so.

## Deadly shark

At 10 ft (3 m) long, the bull shark is one of the largest sharks in the world. Known for its aggressive nature, this predator specializes in hunting in shallow, muddy, coastal water. Bull sharks have been spotted 2,500 miles (4,000 km) upstream on the Amazon River.

## Water monkey

The arowana feeds mainly on fish. However, it can also leap up to 6½ ft (2 m) out of the water to snatch birds, bugs, or other prey. Because of this unique behavior, locals refer to this species as the "water monkey."

*Distinctive metallic blue and orange stripe*

## Tetras

Just ¾ in (2 cm) long, neon tetras are bright little freshwater fish found commonly in home aquaria all over the world. However, their natural habitat is in the Amazon River. The first pet tetras were taken from this river in the 1930s. They are bred in captivity today, with nearly 20 million being sold every year in the United States alone.

# Ancient civilizations

People have lived in the Amazon region for at least 11,000 years. For a long time, scientists thought the region was an untouched wilderness, but new evidence shows that large settlements existed even in the densest parts of the jungle. The civilizations that grew up around the edge of the rain forest left the greatest mark. They included the mighty Inca Empire of the Andes.

### Marajoara pottery

This jar contained the ashes of a person who died about 1,000 years ago and was made by the Marajoara people. They are named after Marajó Island, which, located at the Amazon River's mouth, was the center of their civilization. Much of what is known about them comes from their pottery.

### Cliff burial

This 500-year-old mummy was buried in a cave carved into a cliff in the Peruvian Andes. The cold, dry air in the Andean mountains has preserved several mummies. They belonged to a culture known as the Chachapoyans, also called Warriors of the Clouds because they lived in cloud forests in an area located in present-day Peru.

*Buildings made from stone blocks*

## Cloud city

Shown here are the ruins of a walled city called Kuelap, in the cloud forests of Peru, above the Amazon Basin. The Chachapoyans built this city in the 6th century CE, fortifying it to defend against invaders. However, the Inca—from the other side of the Andes—conquered the Chachapoyans in the 15th century. When the Spanish took over the region a century later, Kuelap was eventually abandoned.

*Ruins surround a reconstructed house at Kuelap*

*Earrings represent a chief figure*

*Hammered and flattened pure gold*

## Made of gold

The Muisca people, who lived in the mountains of Colombia, made this gold figure. In one ritual, a Muisca chief was covered in gold dust, which he washed off in a sacred mountain lake. Priests threw other gold artifacts into the lake as gifts to the goddess who was believed to live there. These rituals would eventually give rise to the myth of *El Dorado*, the legendary kingdom of gold.

## The great Inca

Machu Picchu, seen below in ruins, is a city built by the once-powerful Inca Empire in the Andes, about 155 miles (250 km) north of the Amazon River's source. It was built around 1450 as a retreat for the Inca emperor Pachauti.

## Ciudad Perdida

The Ciudad Perdida, or "lost city"—located on the northernmost tip of the Andes range in Colombia—lay forgotten until the 1970s. No one knows who built it, but archeologists think it is around 1,400 years old. The city has terraced fields and paved roads. Nearly 5,000 people may have lived there.

# Discovery and conquest

In 1494, Spain and Portugal agreed to divide the "new world" in two parts by drawing a vertical line halfway between North America and Europe. Only later did they realize that the line went right through the Amazon Basin. A Spanish army conquered the Inca Empire, creating a territory called Peru. Meanwhile, Portuguese colonists settled at the mouth of the Amazon River, eventually creating the country of Brazil.

### Amazons
In 1542, Spanish explorer Francisco de Orellana became the first European to travel all the way down the Amazon River to the ocean. His men were attacked by female warriors—known as Amazons in Greek mythology—and he gave their name to the river.

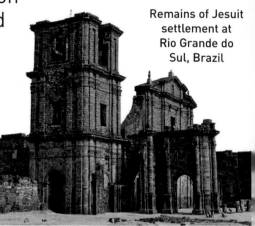

Remains of Jesuit settlement at Rio Grande do Sul, Brazil

### A new religion
The first Europeans who traveled in the Amazon region included Jesuit priests, sent to convert the local people to Christianity. Some of these priests founded churches—later called missions—in the jungle. Many of the region's first modern towns grew around these sites.

### Upstream explorer
In 1637, Portuguese explorers made it all the way upstream from the mouth of the river to present-day Ecuador. Portuguese explorer Pedro Teixeira led the expedition, overseeing 1,270 men in 47 canoes. For the men, it was hard work paddling against the current, and the journey took almost a year to complete.

Statue of Pedro Teixeira in Belém, Brazil, where his journey began

### Slave trade
The European colonists brought African slaves to the Amazon region's mines and plantations to replace local workers who were dying in their thousands from disease and overwork. Between 1550 and 1880, nearly four million Africans ended up in Brazil.

*Many slaves worked in mines, collecting diamonds from broken rocks*

## Rubber boom

In the 1880s, the Amazon region became the world center for rubber production—this period became known as the "Rubber Boom". Businessmen took over large areas of rain forest, and forced local people to work. These rubber barons became very rich; however, the boom only lasted for 30 years, as rubber had begun to be produced in other parts of the world.

## Seeking cinnamon

Early European explorers were looking for spices, which were very valuable in the 16th century. In 1541, Spanish explorer Gonzalo Pizarro heard about a Valley of Cinnamon located to the east of the Andes. He went looking for it, in the hope of becoming wealthy, but returned empty handed.

*Strong beak cracks open nuts*

## Explorers' species

Many of the Amazon's animals are named after naturalists and scientists who led expeditions into the rain forest. For example, the Amazon river dolphin, *Inia geoffrensis*, was named after the French researcher Étienne Geoffroy Saint-Hilaire; Spix's macaw was named after the German biologist Johann Baptist von Spix.

*Long snout grabs slippery fish*

Amazon River dolphin

Spix's macaw

# Myths

The Amazon rain forest is home to many myths and legends. Some ancient stories revolve around good and evil forest spirits, while other myths arose around the time the first Europeans reached the rain forest. Many European fortune seekers heard stories about lost cities and treasures. They never found anything, but the legends lived on, adding more magic to this incredible region.

### Phantom boa

In the rain forest's western parts, many locals believe in the legend of Sachamama, the "spirit mother" of the jungle who looks like a huge snake. People often mistake her body for a fallen tree trunk. Sachamama is considered to be a kind spirit, but will rise up and eat any person who steps on her.

*Armored scales on fish*

### Banished fish

Legend has it that the arapaima (also called pirarucu), the Amazon's biggest fish, is a warrior banished by the gods. The warrior, Pirarucu, was cruel to the villagers, so the gods taught him a lesson. On a stormy fishing trip, Pirarucu was too proud to seek shelter, so was struck by lightning, which turned him into the fish.

## Sacred cassava

The cassava root—known as mandioca to the people of the Amazon rain forest—is thought to be a gift from the gods. Legend has it that a chief's unmarried daughter was made pregnant by the gods. She gave birth to a pale-skinned girl named Mani. Sadly, Mani died on her first birthday, and a strange new plant grew from her grave. This plant was the delicious mandioca.

Postage stamp from Brazil showing the mandioca legend

## Sorcerer tree

Many Amazon villages regard the largest and oldest lupuna tree in the area as a "sorcerer tree." It is believed that the tree can punish bad people by giving them a terrible stomach ache. Some people leave the clothes and possessions of their enemies at the base of the trunk, in the hope that the tree will make them suffer. The sap of the tree is also used to make poisons.

Young lupuna tree

## Quest for gold

Gold was common in the Andes, and the Inca and other native people made many objects from it, like this mask from Colombia. Many European explorers came to the Americas hoping to find *El Dorado*—literally "the golden one"—hidden in the forest. However, no one could find this mythical kingdom.

## Owl spirit

The Amazon rain forest's owls are said to embody the spirit of the Moon goddess Chia. According to an ancient myth, the god of farming, Chibchacum, turned Chia into an owl because she made people very lazy and badly behaved.

*Velvety wings absorb sound and allow owl to fly silently*

## Lost city of the Inca

In the 16th century, after the Spanish conquered the Inca Empire, the Inca fled their cities. But a rumor spread that an army moved to a hidden city called Vilcabamba. Many lost Inca towns have been rediscovered since, like Huinay Huayna (below) in 1941. However, no one has identified Vilcabamba, although some archeologists think that a site called Espíritu Pampa is, in fact, the lost city.

*Stone walls have survived erosion*

# Traditional life

Millions of people lived in the Amazon region before the European conquests of the 16th century. There are about a million indigenous Amazonians left today, although some tribes only have a few hundred members. Many follow the ways of their ancestors, gathering things they need from the forest.

## Magic and medicine
Seen here is a shaman from the Kamentsá tribe of Colombia. A shaman is both a priest and a medicine man. Many Amazonians believe in magic, and if someone becomes sick, they are taken to a shaman for herbal medicines made from forest plants and for rituals that are believed to help in healing.

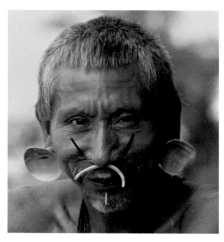

## Uncontacted tribes
This man belongs to the Matis tribe, which lives in the far west of the Amazon region. The tribe first made contact with Brazilian government officials in 1978. The Matis had no natural defenses against diseases common in the rest of the world and about 80 percent of them died from viral infections caught from outsiders.

*Arrows used to shoot monkeys in trees*

## Hunting and gathering
These hunters show their skill with long bows made from wood cut from forest trees. The men belong to the Awá tribe, one of the smallest communities living in the Amazon rain forest. There are about 450 Awá living in Brazil's northeastern Amazon region—around 100 are nomadic and avoid contact with outsiders. They move regularly to new camps, where they gather fruits and hunt animals.

## Following rituals

Young Amazonian men often participate in ancient ritual dances. Every year, the tribes of the Xingu area, located in the southeastern part of the Amazon region, gather for a festival known as *Quarap*. During the event, the tribes organize dances, rituals, and wrestling matches to honor their dead ancestors.

*Chief youth leads the dance*

*Body painted with natural dyes*

*Leg bindings strengthen ankles for wrestling*

## Traditional craft

The Amazon region's indigenous people know how to make everything they need from materials found in the forest. This craftsman from the Yanomami tribe, which lives on the border of Venezuela and Brazil, is making a basket from leaves and vines collected from the forest. Yanomami families live in large shared homes made of logs, dried palm fronds, and other materials.

*Basket is lined with thick leaves*

## River food

The Amazon River and its tributaries are an important source of food for the local people. These fishermen are from the Yawalapiti tribe that lives along the Xingu River. They catch fish by spearing them using bows and arrows. The fish are stored in nets and dried in sunlight so that they can be eaten later.

## Cooking meals

It is traditional for the women of the Amazon region to prepare food. Often, enough food is made for the whole village to eat at once. This woman from the Mawé tribe is roasting guarana seeds in a giant clay dish over a wood fire. Guarana is similar to coffee, and Mawé hunters eat the seeds when they go on long expeditions into the jungle. The Mawé tribe now sells guarana products all over the world.

# Modern Amazonia

Most people in the Amazon region lead normal lives, from watching sports to going to school. Traditional homes stand next to modern buildings in big cities, such as Manaus, Brazil. Yet even here, you are never more than 6 miles (10 km) from the rain forest, and river boats are often the best way to travel between towns and cities.

### Beach resort
The Amazon region has a beach resort 900 miles (1,450 km) away from the ocean. Located at Ponta Negra—on the edge of Manaus, Brazil—bathers take a dip in the Rio Negro, home to Amazon River dolphins and many fish. Lifeguards keep watch over the swimmers, but also look out for caimans.

*Medical boat belongs to the Peruvian navy*

MARINA DE GUERRA DEL PERU

302

### Floating hospital
It can take a long time to get to a hospital in remote parts of the Amazon rain forest. Hospital ships, such as the one shown above, make regular visits to isolated villages in the forest so that ill or injured people can see a doctor and receive treatment. In emergencies, faster river ambulances are used to take patients to the nearest city hospital.

### Carnival culture
These jaguar dancers are performing at a carnival in Parintins, a Brazilian city located beside the Amazon River. A carnival is a party that can be enjoyed by thousands of people from all around the world over several days. Big cities in Brazil have a strong tradition of carnivals, merging African and European traditions with native American culture.

### Amazon communication
Rain forests grow in very sunny places—and these solar panels are using that sunlight to supply electricity for a village in the Amazon rain forest. The electricity powers computers and charges mobile phones. Telecommunication masts on the riverbanks transmit telephone calls and Internet signals.

## River village

Most Amazonian villages are built beside the river. Houses are placed high on the riverbank so they do not flood when the water level of the river is high. Seen here is an unusual village called Belén in Iquitos, Peru. The houses—attached to poles driven into the river bed—float on the river itself, rising and falling with the water.

*Roof thatched with dried palm leaves*

## Soccer city

The Arena da Amazônia stadium is a recent addition to the skyline of Manaus. It was built for the 2014 FIFA World Cup. The stadium's design was inspired by the straw baskets woven by people in the region. The climate of Manaus is very hot and humid, so the stadium's ventilation system, shaded areas, and its light-colored structure help to keep the spectators reasonably comfortable.

## Schooling

Traditional Amazonian villages do not have schools. Children just play until they are old enough to help their parents with tasks. Without basic literacy skills, they cannot find jobs when they are adults. The Brazilian government is building more schools to help solve this problem.

# Getting around

The land is heavily forested in the Amazon region, so the long, wide rivers are ideal for traveling long distances. Even though modern highways now cut through the rain forest, and aircraft connect remote villages with the rest of the world, most of the people living in this region get around by boat, just as they have done for thousands of years.

### Just walk!

Away from the river, the only way to travel through the jungle is by foot. Even the toughest off-road vehicles cannot make their way through the undergrowth and fallen trees. The tourists seen here are taking a short stroll. For longer journeys, travelers need to have a machete to cut through bushes that block their way.

### On the road

In the 1970s, the Brazilian government cut a 3,000-mile (5,000-km) roadway from the Atlantic Coast through the Amazon rain forest to the border with Peru. This Trans-Amazonian Highway is still unfinished, but it has allowed road traffic, and even loggers, right into the heart of the rain forest.

## Bridges

The only road bridge in the Amazon river system crosses the Rio Negro near the city of Manaus, Brazil. Opened in 2011 and 11,800 ft (3,595 m) wide, it had to be high enough for ocean-going cargo ships and the Amazon's ferries to travel to Manaus's port—the region's main transportation hub.

## Riding on horseback

Sure-footed horses and mules are the best way to travel in the foothills of the Andes. Before horses were brought to the region by 16th-century European explorers, Andean people used llamas to carry cargo. However, llamas are not strong enough to carry humans.

*Float allows plane to land on water*

## Air travel

The calm waters of the Amazon River make a good runway for seaplanes. The largest Amazonian cities, such as Manaus and Iquitos, have full-sized airports, but small aircraft, as shown, can fly to remote communities far from any city. Inland, away from the river, skilled pilots land planes on airstrips cut from the forest.

## Going for a paddle

The traditional method of travel on the Amazon Basin's many rivers is to paddle a canoe. They may be carved out from logs, or made from planks of wood, such as balsa. Balsa trees grow across the region, and their wood is lightweight and ideal for canoes and rafts.

# Deforestation

The biggest threat to the Amazon rain forest is deforestation, a process in which trees are cleared, leaving nowhere for the wildlife to live. The forest is being cut down for logging, road building, and to make way for farms. If cleared, the rain forest will never grow back in the same way. Today, strict laws limit deforestation in some parts, although other areas continue to be cleared.

2002

2012

### Satellite surveillance

About a fifth of the Amazon rain forest has been cut down in the last 40 years. The Brazilian government uses satellite images to monitor the rate at which the rain forest is being cleared. The satellites can see changes in the color of the ground, which indicates where trees have been cut down. The images above track deforestation in a section of the rain forest between 2002 and 2012.

### Divisive road

The building of roads is one of the main causes of deforestation. Roads were first cut into the rain forest in the 1970s to help poor people from Brazil's cities to settle in the Amazon region to start a new life. The roads also divide up the forest, making it difficult for many animals to move around as much as they need.

*Lumber being transported from the rain forest*

### Logging

Another major cause of deforestation is logging. The hardwood trees of the Amazon rain forest are used for making furniture that is sold around the world. The loggers cut down a few of the largest trees and then move on to another area.

## Secondary forest

Once the primary, or original, rain forest has been cut down, a secondary forest starts to grow. This has fewer trees and only some of the animals that once thrived in the primary forest. In time, creepers and epiphytes begin to grow in the secondary forest. Many rain forest plants need animals to spread their seeds, and because many of the original animals have disappeared, many of the plants they supported will never return naturally.

Primary forest has a thick canopy, an understory of bushes, and a diverse animal population

After deforestation, cut logs are burned to clear the ground

Grasses and other plants appear

Small trees and shrubs start to grow

Secondary forest has a thinner canopy and fewer plants growing underneath

## Slash and burn

A helicopter carrying environmental officers (right) is flying in to arrest thieves who have cleared trees illegally for farming. The main method of clearing the forest is called slash and burn, a process in which trees are cut up and burned. The ash makes the soil a little more fertile, but only for a few years.

# Mining and damming

The Amazon region is home to millions of people and to some of the world's biggest cities. In order to fuel the cities' quick growth, the region's largest rivers have been dammed to generate electricity, and enormous mines have been dug for metals and useful minerals. There is still room for more dams, and the Amazon Basin is thought to contain vast, untapped reserves of minerals. The big question is whether the rain forest is more valuable than the rich resources it holds.

## Gold rush

There are gold rushes happening all over the Amazon region, with people clearing the forest to look for gold in the rocks underneath. Miners crush the rocks and wash water through them; if they are lucky, this carries away the dust and sand to reveal grains of shiny gold.

## River port

The city of Belém, located near the Amazon River's mouth, has been a very important port in Brazil for hundreds of years. The large market hall, seen on the left, was built beside the port in the 19th century. It sells fish caught from the river, as well as fruits and other products transported downstream from the forest.

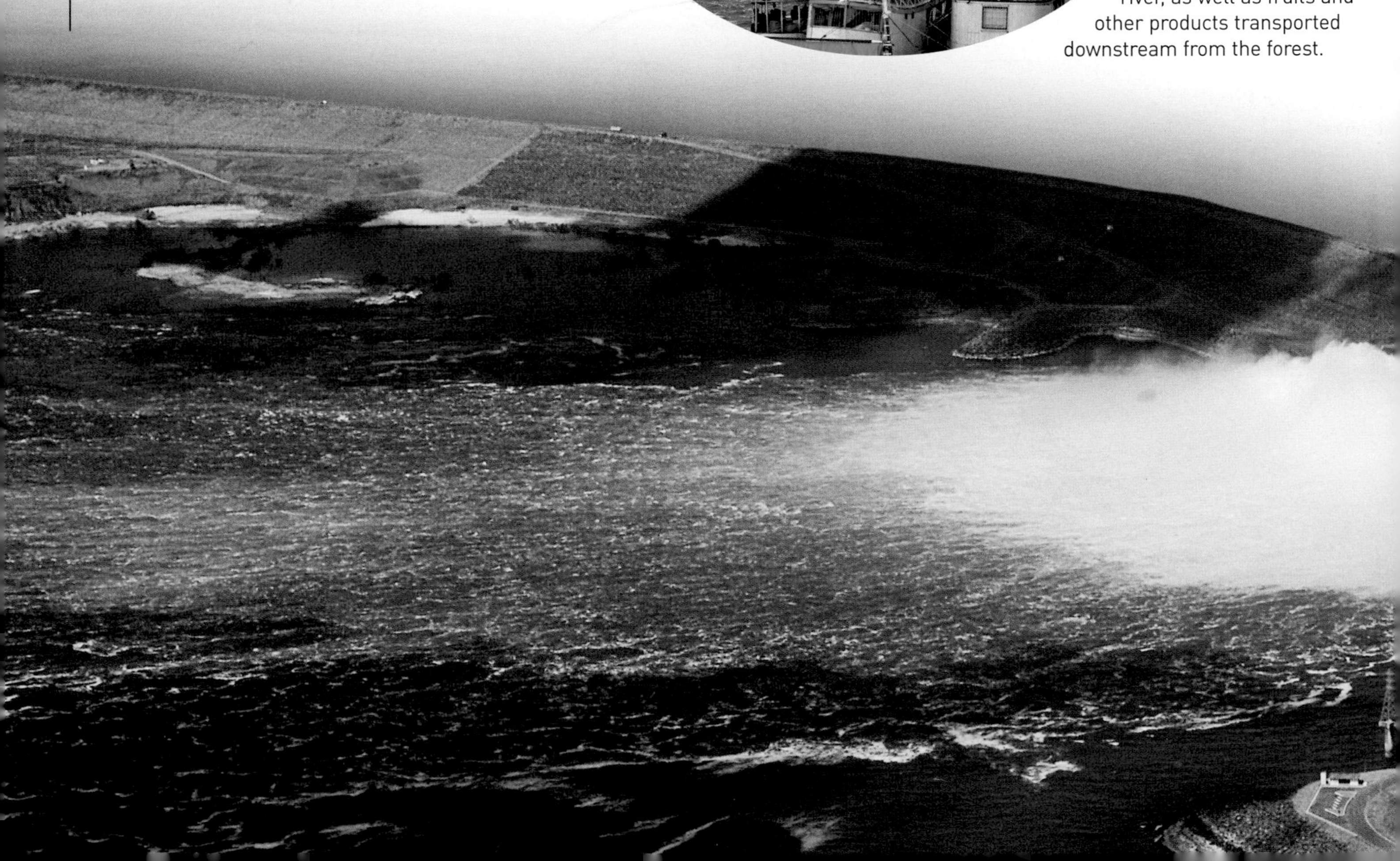

### Mighty mine
The Carajás Mine in Brazil is the largest iron ore mine in the world. About 3,000 people work there, digging out rock that contains iron and other metals. Once all the ore has been dug out, the mine will be filled and a new rain forest will be planted to cover the bare ground.

### Carrying oil
This pipe is carrying crude oil pumped from a well in the rain forests of Ecuador. This valuable resource will be used to make fuel, chemicals, plastic, and medicines. However, pipes and wells can leak, and the spilled oil pollutes the area's rivers, damaging wildlife and causing health problems for those who live in the forests.

### Growing fuel
Brazil is the world's leading producer of sugar cane. Raw sugar from the cane is used to make ethanol, a plant-based alternative for non-renewable fuels, such as coal. Biofuels such as ethanol are thought to be environmentally friendly, but creating sugar cane plantations means cutting down forests, or using land that could be used to grow food crops.

### Battle for land
Many mines, dams, and oil wells occupy land in the Amazon region that belongs to indigenous tribes. These people sometimes protest, so the government must consider the benefits of industry alongside the interests of the indigenous people, and what is good for the environment.

### Damming the river
The Amazon Basin's largest dam—the Tucuruí Dam in Brazil—provides electricity for about 13 million people. However, when it was finished in 1984, it created an enormous reservoir that flooded parts of the rain forest and forced thousands of people to move out of the area. Still, dams such as these also have some environmental benefits, as they help produce electricity without releasing carbon dioxide. Today, nearly all of Brazil's electricity is generated in this manner.

Sluice gates control water flow

# Endangered species

Small patches of the Amazon rain forest have remained unchanged for two million years. Today, nearly three million species of plant and animal may be living there. Yet, as human activity continues to damage the rain forest, a number of species are running out of places in which to survive, and many of these species are in danger of becoming extinct.

## Pacarana

This shy, leaf-eating animal is the last surviving relative of giant, 10-ft- (3-m-) long rodents that lived in the Amazon region about eight million years ago. Small gangs of three or four pacaranas climb through the trees, using their long whiskers to feel their way. This species is becoming scarce because the forests of the western Amazon in which they live are being cut down by farmers.

## Blue birds

The hyacinth macaw is the largest parrot in the Amazon rain forest. It is about 3 ft (1 m) long from its hooked beak to the tip of its long tail feathers. There are now fewer than 6,500 of these birds left in the wild. Its size and bright-blue plumage make this species a tempting target for bird trappers, who sell the parrots as pets.

*Termite hill*

## Maned sloth

Living in the Atlantic Forest, southeast of the main Amazon Basin, the maned sloth moves slowly through the trees, so as not to attract attention. It never cleans its fur, and the algae growing in it lends its hair a green tinge. They are endangered because they are hunted for food, and the trees in which they live are being cut down by loggers.

## English monkey

Local people call the uakari monkey the English monkey because it looks like a sunburned tourist. Living in the trees above flooded forests in Peru, they only climb to the ground in search of seeds when the floodwater has drained away. Hunters can spot these monkeys when they are near the water, so their population is now in decline.

*Redness of face indicates strength to other monkeys*

## White-blotched ray

White-blotched rays live on pebbly riverbeds where they hunt for snails and crabs. They live only in the Xingu River in Brazil, which meets the Amazon River near its mouth. A new electricity-generating dam that is being built across the Xingu will make the river deeper. This may reduce feeding areas and could lead the rays on a path to extinction.

## Giant anteater

The giant anteater rips open the nests of ants and termites and licks up the insects inside with its sticky tongue. At 24 in (60 cm) long, the tongue is one of the longest in the animal kingdom. However, the anteater is vulnerable to extinction, partly because it is too slow to run away from forest fires, which are becoming more common in the region.

*Black-and-white stripes on flank*

*Long arms help monkey to move from tree to tree*

# Modern industry

The Amazon Basin provides many Amazonians with jobs. This helps local communities to build homes, schools, and hospitals, so they can lead comfortable lives. The biggest industry in the region is agriculture and other types of food production. In the future, industries may grow around new products the forest holds.

Palm oil and fruits

## Palm oils

The fruits of palm trees are a traditional food for some Amazonians, but they are also grown for the oil they contain. The oil is used in products such as salad dressings, washing powder, and even in fuels. If managed correctly, palm oil plantations do not damage natural habitats. However, there have been many cases in which palm oil farms have caused environmental problems in the Amazon region because of widespread deforestation.

## Fishing

The Amazon River provides fish for millions of people. The largest fish, the arapaima, is regarded as a delicacy because it has few bones in it and can be cut into thick steaks. But so many wild arapaimas have been taken from the river that the Brazilian government has made it illegal to catch them. Today, arapaimas are raised in fish farms—areas of the river that are surrounded by nets and stocked with fish.

## Soybean farming

This huge farm in the cerrado grasslands south of the Amazon rain forest grows only soybeans. Farms like this dot many parts of the Amazon region. Soybeans are used all over the world to make vegetarian foods and to feed cattle, chickens, and other livestock. Brazil is the world's largest producer of soybeans.

## Medicinal plants

This researcher is talking to a local shaman, or medicine man, to find out which plants he uses to make traditional medicines. The drug curare was discovered in an Amazonian plant. Tribes in the forest traditionally used it as a poison, but in the 1940s, surgeons began to use it to relax patients' muscles during surgery.

*Combine harvester cuts the soy plant and removes the beans*

## Cattle ranches

There are about 10 million cattle in the Amazon region and many millions more in the surrounding hills. Cattle ranches—which include land for growing corn to feed the cattle—are the major cause of deforestation in the area. The problem is made worse when farmers convert ranches into soy plantations, as they must then clear another area of forest for their cattle to graze.

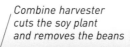

# Conservation

The Amazon rain forest needs protection from the harm caused by human activities. Scientists try and figure out how wildlife survives so that animals can be better cared for. Conservationists work to repair and protect habitats, while lawyers and politicians set rules for people to live in the forest without causing damage to it.

### Replanting
When a tall tree falls down in the forest, it leaves a gap that is filled by other plants. Eventually a new tree fills the space in the canopy. Scientists have observed this process and are trying to re-create it. The plants grown in the reforestation nursery above will be used to replenish the Atlantic Forest.

### Applying science
The two scientists here—known as ecologists—are looking for plant samples during a research project in the Peruvian Amazon. Their important research shows the damage that is caused when humans alter the natural habitat.

### Product bans
These activists are protesting against illegal logging. In 1975, an international ban was introduced on buying and selling endangered species and rain forest products, including hardwood logs from the Amazon rain forest. Sadly, many criminals continue to ignore the ban.

## Conservation sites

Many storks and egrets migrate to the Pantanal wetland every year. If this area were drained to make way for fields, these birds would have nowhere to live. The best way to protect animal species is to conserve their habitats. But today, only 2 percent of the Pantanal is protected in reserves.

*Wood storks arrive from their wintering grounds*

## Saving tribes

The traditional cultures of the Amazon region also need to be saved. A fifth of the rain forest belongs to different tribes that have lived in the area for thousands of years. Statistics show that there is less deforestation in tribal areas than in the rest of the rain forest. Still, big portions of tribal land have been taken over illegally by farmers.

## Traffic sign

With roads being built through the forest, road signs are a new addition to the Amazon region. This one warns drivers to look out for anteaters that may walk onto the road. Anteaters are slow-moving creatures that may not be able to get out of the way of fast-moving vehicles. This species is endangered, and road signs are one way to help it survive.

## Promoting awareness

In 1989, when the problems of deforestation first became known, tribal chiefs from across the rain forest and the rest of North and South America met in Altmira, Brazil, on the banks of the Xingu River. They drew attention to the problems threatening the region. The English musician Sting (far right) also attended the gathering.

# Ecotourism

Tourists pay to visit the Amazon rain forest, and the money they pay goes to the local people and toward conservation programs. Turning the rain forest into a world-class tourist attraction is more beneficial than cutting it down to build cities and farms. This region's vacation industry is a prime example of ecotourism, since the hotels and facilities used by the visitors do not create pollution or damage natural habitats.

## Handicrafts

Local people in the Amazon region use latex from the trees to make natural rubber, which is used to make souvenir masks, such as the one above. Selling handicrafts to tourists is an important source of income for people who live in remote parts of the region.

*Hotel built on stilts in the river*

## Forest resort

Ecotourists stay in comfortable hotels, known as lodges. The buildings are designed to be highly energy-efficient so they do not use a lot of fuel, which has to be brought in by boat. Waste is also kept to a minimum.

## Guided tours

Most visitors to the Amazon rain forest come to see the wildlife. Local guides take tourists on walks through the rain forest or on boat tours. The tourists travel in canoes, not speedboats, since high-speed vessels create waves that would damage the riverbanks. Some guided tours take place at night, when caimans and other nocturnal animals are active.

*Bridge made from forest wood and plant fibers*

## Meeting the locals

Tour groups visit villages, where the residents show off their way of life, such as how they use forest plants to make the things they need. The visits are a chance for Amazonians to make money selling traditional products to visitors.

*Straight sticks sharpened into arrows*

## Saving the animals

Tourists in the Amazon rain forest can help park rangers to care for endangered animals before they are released into the wild. Visitors to Peru are seen here feeding milk to baby manatees. This example of ecotourism helps raise money so that more of the rare manatees can be raised and protected.

*Binoculars for viewing wildlife*

## Walking among the trees

Walkways like this rope walkway, in addition to viewing platforms built in large trees, are the best way to see the rain forest's birds, monkeys, and specialized plants that live high up in the canopy, out of sight from the forest floor.

# Farming

Many fruits and nuts eaten the world over come from forest plants. In the Amazon rain forest, local people have been growing their own crops for centuries, using only traditional farming methods. Today, conservation programs are helping them to develop sustainable methods so that they can grow extra crops to sell. Sustainable farms make money for the Amazon communities without causing any damage to the natural habitats.

## Açái palm
The açaí palm tree grows naturally in the swampy forests near the Amazon River's mouth. Locals harvest the tree for the soft, edible palm hearts inside its young stems. The berries also taste good, and locals use them to make juices.

## Making rubber
Here a farmer is cutting a notch in a rubber tree to release a liquid called latex. This is used to make natural rubber, which is harvested on sustainable farms in the Amazon region. Making things from natural rubber creates much less pollution than artificial rubber—the most common type of rubber, made from petroleum oil.

## Agroforestry

The Amazonian farmers above are raking out chiles to dry in the sunshine. These chile peppers come from a rain forest farm in the eastern Brazilian town of Tomé-açu. This farming community was set up by Japanese settlers 90 years ago. When the local pepper crop was killed by pests, the people of Tomé-açu decided to replant the forest trees and grow crops in their shade. This type of farming is called agroforestry.

Bananas

## Jungle fruits

Although from southeast Asia, bananas are also grown in South America. The first pineapples came from the forests near the Pantanal wetland. Passion fruit is another Amazon plant, and the region was also home to the first tomatoes, peppers, and chiles.

Pineapple

Passion fruit

Coffee beans

## Growing coffee

More than 6½ million tons (6 million metric tons) of coffee beans are sold across the world every year, and some of it is grown in the Amazon rain forest. Farmers grow coffee beans on small bushes that are planted among the main forest trees. Rain forest coffee is also good for the environment.

Coffee plant berries

*Five beans grow inside a tough pod*

## Brazil nuts

Despite the name, these large, tasty nuts are grown all over the Amazon region, not just in Brazil. Wild Brazil nut trees grow along riverbanks. The nuts, which are the trees' seeds, drop to the ground in a round pod. Forest rodents eat some nuts and bury the rest for later. Some of the buried nuts grow into new trees.

## Cocoa

Chocolate comes from cocoa beans, which grow wild in the Amazon rain forest. Native American people were using chocolate in food hundreds of years before it became a popular treat around the world. Today, most of the world's cocoa is grown in West Africa, but it can be grown on rain forest farms.

# Amazon wonders

The Amazon region is a collection of many wonders. The mountains around the Amazon Basin were home to the most advanced civilizations in the Americas prior to the arrival of the Europeans. There are also incredible natural features down in the vast lowlands, as well as historic cities in which modern life and architecture mix with the wild Amazon rain forest.

### Iquitos
This Peruvian city is one of the most remote places on Earth. In the early 1900s, it became a major center in the rubber industry. However, even today, its 420,000 inhabitants cannot leave town by road. They either have to get a boat downriver or catch a plane. The city is 2,235 miles (3,600 km) from the ocean, but the Amazon River is still deep enough here for oceangoing ships to dock in the city's harbor.

### Mount Roraima
According to local folklore, Mount Roraima in the Guiana Highlands is the stump of a huge tree that bore all the fruits in the world until it was cut down by a demon. The mountain's rocks are 2 billion years old and were formed when South America was still connected to Africa.

### Tumucumaque National Park
This nature reserve is the world's largest national park; it is bigger than Belgium.

### Anavilhanas Archipelago
This is the largest archipelago of river islands in the world. It is a collection of 400 forested islands on the Rio Negro, upstream from the Brazilian city of Manaus.

### Rio Negro Bridge
Completed in 2010, this 2.2 mile (3.6 km) bridge, located on the Rio Negro, is the first major road bridge on the Amazon River system.

## Manaus

The Teatro Amazonas opera house was built in 1884 and is still a famous landmark in the Brazilian city of Manaus. It was paid for with money from the rubber industry, the same industry that made Manaus the largest city in the Amazon Basin. Manaus is located at the meeting point of the Amazon River and the Rio Negro.

## Pantanal

The Pantanal is the world's largest wetland. It forms in a hollow basin in the Brazilian Highlands that fills with rainwater flowing down from the surrounding hills. The water never gets more than about 16½ ft (5 m) deep.

## Valle de la Luna

Meaning the Valley of the Moon, the Valle de la Luna is a desert region filled with tall rock towers. The towers were created by erosion that washed away the softer clays that once filled the valley. This valley is close to La Paz, the capital city of Bolivia. They are both located on the Altiplano, a high plateau west of the Amazon Basin.

## Sacred Valley

The Sacred Valley in the Peruvian Andes was the heartland of the Inca Empire. The Inca used these ancient, man-made pools to produce salt. The rest of the valley was used to grow corn, which was the main food in Inca cooking. The imperial Inca capital was Cuzco, which is located at the southern end of the valley.

## Machu Picchu

The Inca city of Machu Picchu sits high up in the Andes Mountains. It was thought to be a religious center used by the Inca king, but it was abandoned and forgotten after the collapse of the Inca Empire in the 16th century. It lay hidden under jungle until it was rediscovered in 1911.

# Amazon facts

The Amazon region is a place of superlatives. It has the world's largest rain forest, its biggest river system, its largest river island, its widest river mouth, and its biggest tributary. Here are many more facts that show what an incredible place this region is and how record-breaking some of its animals are.

## Mass of life

Biomass is a measure of how many living things exist in an area. Rain forests have the highest biomass of any land habitat. The biomass in one square mile of the Amazon rain forest is equivalent to the weight of two Nimitz-class aircraft carriers used by the US Navy, each of which weighs nearly 100,000 tons.

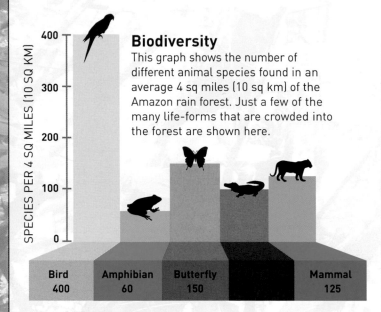

### Biodiversity

This graph shows the number of different animal species found in an average 4 sq miles (10 sq km) of the Amazon rain forest. Just a few of the many life-forms that are crowded into the forest are shown here.

SPECIES PER 4 SQ MILES (10 SQ KM)

| Bird | Amphibian | Butterfly | | Mammal |
|------|-----------|-----------|---|--------|
| 400 | 60 | 150 | | 125 |

### Endangered species

Many Amazonian species are under threat because of damage to their habitat. The international body charged with monitoring endangered species, the International Union for Conservation of Nature (IUCN), has listed 536 animal and 778 plant species as being in danger of extinction in the Amazon region.

Key

*Vulnerable*

*Endangered*

*Critically endangered*

South American manatee

Uakari monkey

Giant anteater

Golden lion tamarin

Pacarana

Giant otter

Rancho Grande harlequin frog

Glaucous macaw

Cherry-throated tanager

## LARGEST ANIMALS

The capybara is the largest rodent in the world. This species lives in the rivers and wetlands of the Amazon region. It can grow to more than 3¼ ft (1 m) in length.

Amazonian macaws are the largest types of parrot in the world. Some species can grow to about 3¼ ft (1 m) in length.

At just over 1 in (3 cm) long, the Amazon rain forest's bullet ants are among the largest ants in the world.

The mighty green anaconda hunts in the wetlands and the forest rivers of the Amazon region, using its muscular coils to squeeze prey to death. At about 16½ ft (5 m) long, it may not be the longest snake in the world (some pythons in Asia are longer), but it is certainly the heaviest— a fully grown anaconda can weigh up to 220 lb (100 kg).

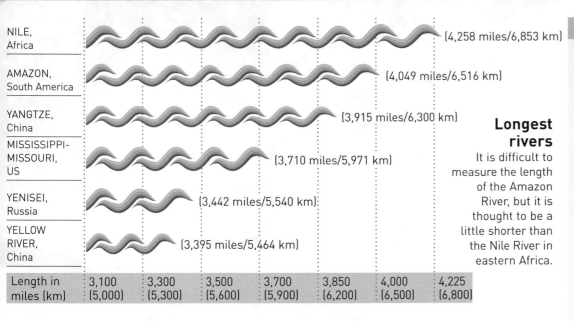

| | | | | | | | |
|---|---|---|---|---|---|---|---|
| NILE, Africa | | | | | | (4,258 miles/6,853 km) | |
| AMAZON, South America | | | | | (4,049 miles/6,516 km) | | |
| YANGTZE, China | | | | (3,915 miles/6,300 km) | | | |
| MISSISSIPPI-MISSOURI, US | | | (3,710 miles/5,971 km) | | | | |
| YENISEI, Russia | | (3,442 miles/5,540 km) | | | | | |
| YELLOW RIVER, China | (3,395 miles/5,464 km) | | | | | | |
| Length in miles (km) | 3,100 (5,000) | 3,300 (5,300) | 3,500 (5,600) | 3,700 (5,900) | 3,850 (6,200) | 4,000 (6,500) | 4,225 (6,800) |

## Longest rivers

It is difficult to measure the length of the Amazon River, but it is thought to be a little shorter than the Nile River in eastern Africa.

## SMALLEST ANIMALS

At just ½ in (1 cm) long, Izecksohn's toad is the smallest frog in the Amazon rain forest.

The tiny white-bellied woodstar is 3 in (8 cm) long.

**RIVER BASIN**

| | |
|---|---|
| Amazon | (3.8 million sq miles/ 6.15 million sq km) |
| Congo | (2.4 million sq miles/ 3.82 million sq km) |
| Mississippi-Missouri | (2 million sq miles/ 3.22 million sq km) |
| Nile | (1.7 million sq miles/ 2.8 million sq km) |
| Ganges | (0.7 million sq miles/ 1.07 million sq km) |

1   2   3   4   5   6
Area of drainage basin (million sq km)

## Largest basin

The Amazon River drains the largest area of any river in the world. The amount of water it collects from its basin is almost twice as much as the Congo River.

## DANGEROUS ANIMALS

The golden poison dart frog of Ecuador is the most toxic vertebrate in the world. Its skin is filled with a powerful poison that protects it from predators. Just touching the frog is enough to make you sick.

The caimans of the Amazon region generally hunt for capybaras and fish, but they have been known to grab people who come too close to the water's edge.

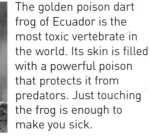

The jaguar has the strongest jaws of any big cat. It can crack skulls and shatter a turtle shell with one bite.

The tropical rattlesnake's venom causes blindness and internal bleeding and makes muscles go limp.

When crowded into a small pool, a school of piranhas can eat a person in minutes.

# Amazon by country

The Amazon Basin covers nine separate countries. Most of the rain forest is located in Brazil, and Peru contains the next biggest section. The remaining 20 percent is divided among the seven other countries.

## KEY

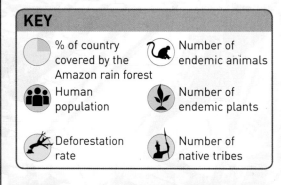

- % of country covered by the Amazon rain forest
- Number of endemic animals
- Human population
- Number of endemic plants
- Deforestation rate
- Number of native tribes

## VENEZUELA

The Llanos wetland and Guiana Highlands are located in this country. Venezuela's main forests are around the Orinoco River, which flows into the Caribbean Sea and is connected to the Amazon River near its source in Brazil.

5.56%    313    30 million

8,007    0.6%

26

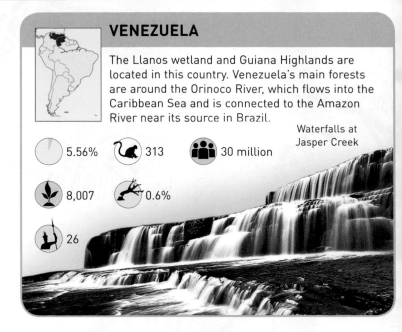

Waterfalls at Jasper Creek

## BRAZIL

The largest country in South America, Brazil is also the fifth most populated nation in the world. More than half of its territory is covered by the Amazon Basin. Seventy percent of the Amazon rain forest is located within its borders.

Iguazu Falls, on the Iguazu River

## ECUADOR

Ecuador gets its name from the Equator, which runs through the middle of the country. The Andes run north to south through the country, dividing the Pacific coastal areas in the west from the Amazon rain forest in the east. The Ecuadorian rain forest is famous for its large areas of flooded forest.

45.7%    383    16 million

4,007    1.9%    27

Cotopaxi, an Andean volcano

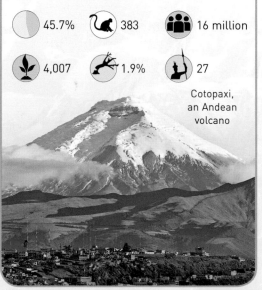

## COLOMBIA

About five percent of the Amazon rain forest is located in the southern part of Colombia. The northern range of the Andes Mountains, which was the site of many important Pre-Columbian cultures, is also found there.

42%    604    48 million    15,366

0.16%    87

Monserrate Sanctuary in Bogotá, the capital city

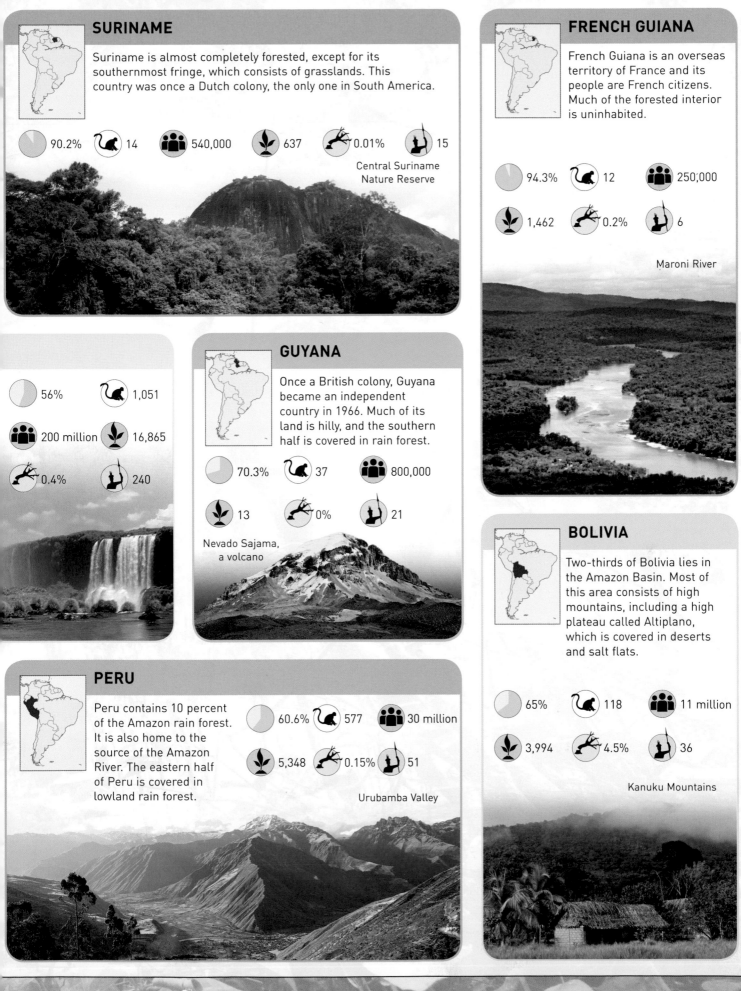

## SURINAME

Suriname is almost completely forested, except for its southernmost fringe, which consists of grasslands. This country was once a Dutch colony, the only one in South America.

90.2%   14   540,000   637   0.01%   15

Central Suriname Nature Reserve

## FRENCH GUIANA

French Guiana is an overseas territory of France and its people are French citizens. Much of the forested interior is uninhabited.

94.3%   12   250,000

1,462   0.2%   6

Maroni River

56%   1,051

200 million   16,865

0.4%   240

## GUYANA

Once a British colony, Guyana became an independent country in 1966. Much of its land is hilly, and the southern half is covered in rain forest.

70.3%   37   800,000

13   0%   21

Nevado Sajama, a volcano

## BOLIVIA

Two-thirds of Bolivia lies in the Amazon Basin. Most of this area consists of high mountains, including a high plateau called Altiplano, which is covered in deserts and salt flats.

65%   118   11 million

3,994   4.5%   36

Kanuku Mountains

## PERU

Peru contains 10 percent of the Amazon rain forest. It is also home to the source of the Amazon River. The eastern half of Peru is covered in lowland rain forest.

60.6%   577   30 million

5,348   0.15%   51

Urubamba Valley

# Glossary

**AGROFORESTRY**
The practice of cultivating agricultural crops among naturally growing trees. Agroforestry helps protect natural habitats.

**AMPHIBIAN**
A class of vertebrate that generally spends part of its life in water and has to keep its skin moist at all times. Frogs and salamanders are amphibians.

**ARID**
Describes an area that is dry all the time.

**ATLANTIC FOREST**
An area of rain forest in Brazil near the coast of the Atlantic Ocean.

**BACTERIA**
Tiny organisms that are far too small to see without a microscope. Most bacteria live in natural habitats and are harmless.

**BASIN**
A hollow area of land surrounded by hills or mountains on at least three sides.

**BIOMASS**
A measure of how much life is contained in an area. Biomass is calculated by adding up the combined weight of all life-forms.

Strawberry poison dart frog, an amphibian

drop their leaves during harsh seasons. Most deciduous trees shed leaves before winter, but in the tropics they drop leaves in the hottest, driest time of the year.

**DEWLAP**
A flap of skin that hangs down from the neck or throat.

**ENDANGERED**
When an animal or other life-form is in danger of becoming extinct.

**ENDEMIC**
A species that occurs naturally in one place and is found nowhere else on Earth.

**EPIPHYTES**
Plants that lack roots and grow on the branches and trunks of other, larger plants.

**HIGHLANDS**
An area of hills, mountains, and plateaux. Most highlands are mountains that have been worn down over millions of years.

**HUMID**
Describes a climate in which the air is full of water vapor.

**INDIGENOUS**
Originating in, or belonging to, a particular place.

**INVERTEBRATE**
An animal without a backbone, such as an insect, snail, or worm. Of all the animal species known to science, at least 97 percent are invertebrates.

**LIANA FOREST**
A forest dominated by lianas—climbing plants that grow out of the ground and snake up around the trunks and branches of trees to reach the sunlight. Lianas use the host tree to support their own weight.

Inflated dewlap on an anole lizard

**CAATINGA**
A type of dry forest found around the edges of the Amazon rain forest. It has sandy soil and is filled with grasses, bushes, and small trees.

**CAECILIAN**
An unusual amphibian that looks like a snake or worm. While most caecilians live on the forest floor, some swim in water.

**CERRADO**
An area of mostly shrubs and grasses that grows around the edge of the Amazon rain forest, where the rainfall is not sufficient for a full forest to grow.

**CLOUD FOREST**
A type of tropical forest that grows on the slopes of mountains. The trees are smaller than those in a lowland jungle, and the area is often covered in fog or mist from low-lying clouds.

**DECIDUOUS**
Describes a process in which something falls off a living body and then regrows later. It is often used to describe trees that

**EVERGREEN**
A tree or other plant that is always covered in leaves. New leaves continue to grow even as old leaves fall off.

**EXTINCT**
When all members of a species have died.

**FLOODED FOREST**
A forest that is flooded with river water so the tree trunks and roots are submerged in water.

**FLOODWATER**
Extra water from a river that overflows the riverbanks and covers nearby land.

**GEOGRAPHY**
A field of science concerned with the study of the lands, features, inhabitants, and phenomena of Earth.

**HABITAT**
A place where a plant or animal lives. Most species are adapted to live in one type of habitat, such as a rain forest.

**LOGGER**
Someone who cuts down trees that are turned into timber products. Some loggers are criminals because they cut down trees that are protected by law.

Liana wrapped around tree trunk

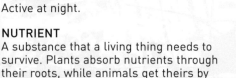
Wandering spider (predator) eats a beetle (prey)

## LOGGING
An industry that provides lumber for construction and paper manufacture. Most of the world's logging is conducted in forests that are grown specially to supply lumber. However, the Amazon rain forest suffers from illegal logging.

## LOWLAND
An area of flat land that is not very far above sea level, the point from which the heights of all land forms are measured.

## MACHETE
A tool with a thick cutting blade. Machetes help to cut a path through thick jungle.

## MARSUPIAL
A type of mammal that carries its young in a pouch on its belly. Most marsupials are from Australia and New Guinea, but a few species also live in the Americas.

## NATIVE
Refers to someone or something from the local area. Native Amazonians belong to communities that have lived in the region for perhaps thousands of years.

## NOCTURNAL
Active at night.

## NUTRIENT
A substance that a living thing needs to survive. Plants absorb nutrients through their roots, while animals get theirs by eating other life-forms. Nutrients include fats and proteins.

## PETROLEUM
Also known as rock oil or crude oil. Petroleum is the thick black liquid that is pumped up from underground at oil wells. It is a complex mixture of chemicals that have been created over many millions of years from the remains of living things. Petroleum is then refined to make fuels, chemicals, plastics, and pharmaceuticals.

## PLATEAU
A flat area high above sea level.

## POLLINATION
The process in which pollen is delivered to a flower by an insect or other animal, or by the wind. Flowers must be pollinated to produce seeds.

## POLLUTION
The process by which human activities introduce harmful substances to the natural environment. Chemicals in the air, water, or soil, as well as too much light or noise, are all forms of pollution.

## POPULATION
In biology, a group of animals of one species that live in a particular area, such as a forest or even a single tree.

## PREDATOR
A hunting animal that catches and kills another animal for food.

## PREHENSILE
A body part that can grasp an object, and so functions like a hand or foot.

## PREHISTORIC
Referring to the time in a culture's history when no historical events were recorded.

## PREY
An animal that is hunted by a predator.

## REPTILE
A class of vertebrate that lays its eggs on land and has a body covered in waterproof scales. Reptiles include snakes, lizards, turtles, and crocodiles.

## RIVER SYSTEM
A network of rivers that collect water from a particular region.

Napo River, a tributary of the Amazon River

## RODENT
A small mammal that has sharp front teeth that are used for gnawing. Rodents include mice, squirrels, and guinea pigs.

## SALT FLAT
A region of land that is covered in a crust of salt crystals.

## SYMBIOSIS
A partnership between two members of different species. Both partners help each other by providing food or protection.

## TIDAL BORE
A tall wave that travels up a river when the tide is very high.

## TRIBUTARY
A small river that flows into a larger one.

## VENOMOUS
Refers to venom, a poison that is injected by an animal into another one. Also used to describe animals that secrete venom.

## VERTEBRATE
An animal that has a backbone.

## VOLCANO
A mountain that develops around a crack in our planet's crust. Hot molten rock erupts out of the crack and spreads over the land as lava.

Reventador volcano, Ecuador

# Index

# Acknowledgments

**Dorling Kindersley would like to thank:** Ashwin Khurana for text editing; Helen Peters for indexing; Dan Green for proofreading; Simon Mumford for illustrating maps; and Sheryl Sadana for editorial assistance.

The publisher would like to thank the following for their kind permission to reproduce their photographs: (Key: a-above; b-below/bottom; c-center; f-far; l-left; r-right; t-top)

1 Dreamstime.com: Ammit. 2 Alamy Images: Cindy Hopkins (cl). Corbis: DPA / Rolf Wilms (cb); Layne Kennedy (b). Dorling Kindersley: The Natural History Museum, London (cl). Dreamstime.com: Amwu (ttl). Getty Images: Photodisc / Alex Cao (tc). Thomas Marent: (tc/Fungus beetle). 2–3 Dreamstime.com: Rinus Baak (tr). 3 Dreamstime.com: 44kmos (tr); Eric Gevaert (c). 4 Alamy Images: Westend61 GmbH (r). Corbis: Hugh Sitton (br). Dreamstime.com: Andrea Poole (t); Isselee (tc); Viktarm (cll); Dolphfyn (cr). 5 SuperStock: Iberfoto (tr). Corbis: Minden Pictures / Murray Cooper (cl). Getty Images: De Agostini (bl). 8 Dreamstime.com: Antares614 (tr). NASA: GSFC (tl). 9 Alamy Images: Lee Dalton (tr). Corbis: Stephanie Maze (br). Photoshot: Imagebroker (cr). 10 Alamy Images: age fotostock / Alvaro Leiva (tr). Dean Jacobs: (tl). 11 Alamy Images: Visual&Written SL (cr). Corbis: Reuters / Bruno Domingos (bl). NASA: (tr). 12 Alamy Images: BrazilPhotos.com (cr); Robert Fried (b). Getty Images: Photographer's Choice (t); Photolibrary (c). 13 Alamy Images: BrazilPhotos.com. Corbis: Minden Pictures / Kevin Schafer (cl). Dreamstime.com: Kschua (tr). 14-15 Corbis: Ultimate Chase / Mike Theiss (b). 14 Alamy Images: Zoonar GmbH (cr). Corbis: Galen Rowell (tl). 15 Alamy Images: David Noton Photography (tr); Martin Harvey (tl). Corbis: Alison Wright (c). 16 Corbis: DPA / Rolf Wilms (c); Theo Allofs (tl). 16-17 SuperStock: Minden Pictures (b). 17 Alamy Images: blickwinkel (tc). Corbis: Reuters / PAULO WHITAKER (cra). Glowimages: jspix (cl). 18 Corbis: Minden

Pictures / Mark Moffett (cra). Thomas Marent: (bl). Photoshot: NHPA (tl). 19 Alamy Images: Jacques Jangoux (br). Corbis: Minden Pictures / Mark Moffett (tr). Thomas Marent: (tr). 20 Alamy Images: Westend61 GmbH (tl). Dreamstime.com: David Davis (c); Steffen Foerster (tr); Lukas Blazek (bc); Hotshotsworldwide (clb). 20-21 Dreamstime.com: Rinus Baak (c). 21 Alamy Images: Images & Stories (bl); Kuttig - Travel (cr). Chris Jiménez: (cl). Dreamstime.com: 44kmos (br); Hotshotsworldwide (tc). Photoshot: NHPA (tr). 22 Corbis: Arte & Immagini srl (cl). Minden Pictures / Thomas Marent (cla); AsiaPix / Disc Pictures (ca); Minden Pictures / Pete Oxford (clb). 22-23 Dreamstime.com: Eric Gevaert (b). 23 Corbis: Minden Pictures / Murray Cooper (r). Photoshot: Picture Alliance (tl). 24 Alamy Images: Amar and Isabelle Guillen—Guillen Photo LLC (bl); Juniors Bildarchiv GmbH (br). Corbis: Kevin Schafer (cra). FLPA: Photo Researchers (tl). 25 Alamy Images: William Mullins (tc). Corbis: Minden Pictures / Pete Oxford (tl). Dreamstime.com: Andrea Poole (br). 26 Alamy Images: Magica (clb/Euchroma gigantea); The Natural History Museum (clb/Titan Beetle). Corbis: Minden Pictures / Christian Ziegler (tl). Thomas Marent: (clb). 26-27 Getty Images: (b). 27 Corbis: Minden Pictures / Piotr Naskrecki (tr). Dorling Kindersley: The Natural History Museum, London (tl, ca). Dreamstime.com: Amwu (br). FLPA: Photo Researchers (cr). Thomas Marent: (crb). 28 naturepl.com: Doug Perrine. 29 Alamy Images: Prisma Bildagentur AG (tc). Corbis: Minden Pictures / Kevin Schafer (clb). Phil Myers, Animal Diversity Web (http://animaldiversity.org): (bl). Science Photo Library: John Devries (br). 30 Photoshot: NHPA (bl). Science Photo Library: Dr Morley Read (br). Jerry Young: (cb). 30-31 Dreamstime.com: Ammit (c). 31 naturepl.com: Nick Garbutt (tr). Rex Features: Gerard Lacz (br). 32 Alamy Images: Nature Picture Library / Pete Oxford (clb). Dreamstime.com: Amwu (bl); Dirk Ercken (c, bc); Isselee (br). FLPA: Photo Researchers (c). 32-33 123RF.com: Morley Read (b). Dreamstime.com: Isselee (b). 33 Angi Nelson: (tl). Dreamstime.com: Isselee (bc,

br); Mgkuijpers (bl). SuperStock: NaturePL (crb). 34 Alamy Images: Joe Blossom (c); Morley Read (tl). Corbis: Minden Pictures / Pete Oxford (tr). Dreamstime.com: Isselee (b); Mgkuijpers (cl). 35 Getty Images: Edelcio Muscat (tc). Igor Siwanowicz: (b). 36 Alamy Images: Juniors Bildarchiv GmbH (tl); WaterFrame (cr). Pittsburgh Zoo & PPG Aquarium: (b). 37 Alamy Images: Joshua Hee (clb). Getty Images: Alexander Safonov (tr); Photo by K S Kong (c). 38 Alamy Images: Heritage Image Partnership Ltd (tl). Getty Images: National Geographic / Gordon Wiltsie (cra). 38-39 Glowimages: Hermes Images (b). 39 Dreamstime.com: Ildipapp (crb); Yeolka (tl). Getty Images: AFP / Mauricio Duenas (cl). 40 123RF.com: rook76 (br). With permission from Sociedad Estatal Correos y Telégrafos, S.A. (tl). Alamy Images: Rolf Richardson (br). Getty Images: Antonello (cra). Science Photo Library: Sheila Terry (clb). 41 Alamy Images: Patrick Pleul / Dpa Picture Alliance Archive (cr). Getty Images: Almir Bindilatti (tl); Photodisc / Alex Cao (tr). naturepl.com: Mark Carwardine (b). 42-43 SuperStock: Iberfoto (b). 42 123RF.com: ammit (br). Artwork (c) Christine Marsh, www.christinemarsh.com: (bl). 43 Alamy Images: Alison Wright (tl). Dreamstime.com: mlorenzphotography (crb). Mauricio Mercadante https://www.flickr.com/photos/mercadanteweb: (ca). Source: Empresa Brasileira de Correios e Telégrafos: (tr). 44 Ardea: Nick Gordon (cl). Alamy Images: Jan Sochor / age fotostock (tr). 44-45 © Survival International: (b). 45 Corbis: Ueslei Marcelino / Reuters (tl, cb). naturepl.com: Luiz Claudio Marigo (tr). Photoshot: (bl). Alamy Images: peruvianpictures.com (cla); Rolf Richardson (br). Photoshot: NHPA (clb). 46-47 Alamy Images: James Davies Photography (b). 47 Alamy Images: Paul Harris / John Warburton-Lee Photography (tl); Paul Schulten / imageBROKER (br). www.brasil.gov.br: Chico Batata / Agecom—AM (cl). 48 Alamy Images: Brasil2 (clb). 48-49 Corbis: Hugh Sitton (b). 49 Alamy Images: Larry Larsen (crb); Carlos Mora (tr). Dreamstime.com: Alex Braga (br). 50 Alamy Images: Ricardo Beliel / BrazilPhotos (b). Getty Images: Donald Nausbaum (cr). NASA: Earth Observatory (tl, cla). 51 Corbis: Reuters (b). 52 Alamy Images: BrazilPhotos. (cr); Nigel Dickinson (tl). 52-53 Science Photo Library: Jacques Jangoux. 53 Alamy Images: Edward Parker (tl); Stock Connection Blue (br). Dreamstime. com: Jfanchin (cr). Getty Images: AFP / Antonio Scorza

(cl). 54 Corbis: Minden Pictures / Roland Seitre (cr). Dreamstime.com: Musat Christian (cl). 55 Alamy Images: Amazon-Images (r); WWPics / Kelvin Aitken (cl); Westend61 GmbH (b). Getty Images: Danita Delimont (tl). 56 Corbis: Reuters / Brazil / Stringer (c). Dreamstime.com: Dolphfyn (cla). 56-57 Corbis: Paulo Fridman (b). 57 Getty Images: AFP / Evaristo Sa (cr). Science Photo Library: Alison Wright (tl). 58 Corbis: Reuters / Mariana Bazo (cra). Getty Images: AFP / Xavier Leoty (b); Mint Images / Frans Lanting (tl). 59 Alamy Images: Sue Cunningham Photographic (clb). Corbis: Demotix / Ik Aldama (t); Minden Pictures / Theo Allofs (tl); Frans Lanting (br). 60 Alamy Images: Cindy Hopkins (tl); Jan Carroll (c); Paul Springett C (bl). 60-61 Getty Images: Nigel Pavitt (c). 61 Getty Images: National Geographic / Richard Olsenius (cr); WIN-Initiative (tl). 62 Corbis: Minden Pictures / Luciano Candisani (b). Photoshot: Nigel Smith (tl). 63 Alamy Images: Ammit (br); MNS Photo (cla); Fernanda Preto (bc). Dreamstime.com: Goodween123 (cl); Viktarm (cra). Getty Images: Kam & Co. (tr); UniversalImagesGroup (tl). 64 123RF.com: Alexandre Braga (bc). Alamy Images: Aaron Chervenak (cb). Dreamstime.com: Anatolii Aleksieiev (c); Debra Law (tr). Getty Images: Alex Robinson (clb). 64-65 Corbis: Minden Pictures / Kevin Schafer. 65 Dreamstime.com: Brizardh (ca); Gunter Hoffmann (tr). 66 Dreamstime.com: Amaiquez (cra); Pablo Hidalgo (crb). 66-67 Corbis: Minden Pictures / Kevin Schafer. 67 Corbis: Minden Pictures / Kevin Schafer (cl). Dreamstime.com: Alslutsky (cra); Feeding White-bellied Woodstar (clb); Mikelane45 (bl); Honourableandbold (crb); Marek Jelínek (crb); Razvani (br). Thomas Marent: (clb/Frog). 68-69 Corbis: Minden Pictures / Kevin Schafer. 68 Dreamstime.com: Attila Jandi (c). 69 123RF.com: Pawel Opaska (c). Corbis: Remi Benali (tr). Dreamstime.com: Kseniya Ragozina (tl). Getty Images: Ariadne Van Zandbergen (tl); Danita Delimont (br). 70-71 Corbis: Reuters / Brazil / Kevin Schafer. 70 123RF.com: Dirk Ercken (tc). Thomas Marent: (br). 71 123RF.com: ammit (br); Morley Read (tr). Dreamstime.com: Kseniya Ragozina (tr).

All other images © Dorling Kindersley
For further information see: www.dkimages.com